ECHOES
LISTENING TO
THE VOICES
IN
SPIRITEDTREES

Author: Michelina Docimo
Artist: Kathy Hirshon

Editor: Rosemary Serluca-Foster
Printmaker: Michael Van der Linden
Book design by ShiftFWD

To my parents and children
and theirs
and theirs
and theirs...

Acknowledgements

I am so thankful to those who have helped make this book on Spirited Trees alive. Without their support, wisdom, inspiration, encouragement, enthusiasm, and simply their existence, this book would not have blossomed into being.

To Kathy Hirshon, the creator of Spirited Trees, for her vision and understanding of something bigger than oneself, yet still humbly One, I am forever grateful for this opportunity of writing my first book. Looking at your trees has helped me listen more deeply. And to her husband, Ken, whose quiet, admiring nod meant more than words.

To each and every one of the individuals whom I interviewed and answered my questions and have become a part of my voice: Sandra E. Angulo, Moses Boone, Dr. Anthony Cernera, Laura DePreta, Monsignor Stephen DiGiovanni, Rabbi Joseph Ehrenkranz, Susan Freeland, Emilio Funicella, Stephen Grasso, Noel Furie, Abdel Metwally, Selma Miriam, Eric Morgan, Wendy Black Nasta, Rainer Schrom, K. Patricia Thrane, and Carlos Vasquez, thank you for your generous time, sharing your stories, and all the work you continue to do to build spirited, sustainable communities.

To my editor, Rosemary Serluca Foster, for her meticulous attention to rhyme, meter, and time, your help in preparing this manuscript for publication has been invaluable.

To printmaker, Michael Van der Linden, for capturing the true and timeless colors and heart of Spirited Trees, thank you truly!

To Naomi Niles and Koldo Barroso of ShiftFWD for nailing a beautiful eBook design on the first try, I am so thankful for your insight, talent, and collaboration.

To my friends who expressed a sincere interest and curiosity in this book, thank you so much for celebrating this accomplishment with me.

To a generous connector, Gene D'Agostino, who introduced me to Richard Friswell, and to Richard, for helping my writing grow.

To my family who knew, and sometimes didn't, that I was writing a book, thank you for not asking questions and letting me be.

And to my husband, Dario, who never complained once of the journals that lay between us late at night, letting me read and write in bed as if I were alone in my own world – your sense of humor and support has been a saving grace. Thank you for listening to me and helping me bring this to fruition.

TABLE OF CONTENTS

Nature is the art of God.
Dante Alighieri

O God,
Whenever I listen to the voice
of anything you have made--
The rustling of the trees,
The trickling of water,
The cries of birds,
The flickering of shadow,
The roar of the wind,
The song of the thunder,
I hear it saying:
God is One!
Nothing can be compared with God!

Rabi'a, eighth century, tr. Charles Upton

INTRODUCTION

The Origin of this Book

      The journey that leads to this very page began in 2009 with my asking a simple question, "May I write for you?" A friend had recommended I contact Richard Friswell, creator and editor of *ARTES Magazine,* an online art magazine. I was told he was looking for new writers, so I emailed a note and a few writing samples. His quick and short reply, "Call me." When we spoke, I told Richard I would love to write a piece about art that focuses on nature and sustainability. "Go for it," he said, opening the door for me to write my first feature on topics that stir my soul and that are an integral part of my DNA. Tracing back just one generation, my family line is made up of people who worked, stewarded, and listened to the land. We are all part of a very old family.

"Now what am I going to write about?" I thought, hanging up the phone.

      With no ideas immediately sparking, I distracted myself by checking email. And there, in my inbox, was the answer—an invitation from the Bartlett Arboretum and Gardens to attend Kathy Hirshon's Spirited Trees opening exhibition that very night! Jung would have called this a "meaningful coincidence" in that Kathy's art epitomizes this symbiotic relationship of nature and culture, a meeting of modern and ancient philosophies. Kathy is a talented artist who embraces creating strong community ties and supporting sustainable living.

      Feeling profoundly guided, I attended the opening and took in the Spirited Trees exhibition, which was comprised of over one hundred painted tree silhouettes, studies, and sketches that led to nine wood panels with human faces deeply etched and burned directly into the bark. Each of the nine panels had a different theme: Receiving, Arriving, Being, Learning, Tending, Creating, Holding, and Listening, representing Kathy's own journey as an artist, but one that is common to all of us. I introduced myself to Kathy and we immediately connected. Even amongst a swarm of attendees, she took time to speak with me and walked me through the panels. But what I also found fascinating was observing others observing the art. Everyone was deeply engaged, connecting and commenting on the unique imagery before them, quite different than being in a stark, silent gallery, where everyone remains solemn, composed.

That night, Spirited Trees inspired conversation about Buddha, Krishna, Moses, and Jesus, about going deeper and deeper into your heart, about cultivating peace, community, and spirit. That night, Spirited Trees encouraged conversation about taboo topics that are continually avoided for fear of offending, for fear of ridicule, for fear of harassment, for fear of fear. That night, fear was defied and those fortunate enough to be present at such a gathering of hope became like robins and doves, their words sprouting wings that moved unabashedly throughout the warmly lit room carrying messages that seemed to be under lock and key for centuries. That night, I was so inspired that I went home and wrote the article in one sitting. That night, the art was so viscerally powerful for me that it occupied my dreams.

After the article in *ARTES* was published, Kathy contacted me to thank me and our conversation of Spirited Trees continued. These candid discussions began to spark a desire within myself to cultivate a book that embraced this message of harmony and hope. The seed was planted.

Over the next few months, I spent time getting to know Kathy and her artwork and learning how the wood panels came to be. I took each panel home, and one by one, I counted the faces, imagined the stories, and discovered universal symbols that evoked a calling to create something that was outside of myself, ultimately manifesting in the form of the accompanying poems that expanded into people. Yes, it required looking deeply within, but by looking outward and to others I was able to continue the open dialogue that had begun on the opening night.

"I had been invited by the Bartlett Arboretum and Gardens to prepare a one-woman art show," said Kathy. By walking the Bartlett's grounds, studying the trees, and talking to visitors, gardeners, and arborists, her creative subject began to reveal itself. On a guided woodland walk Kathy asked a young intern, "Do you see a face in this tree?" He responded, "I see a thousand faces!" The many, many faces began to unveil themselves in the trees and Kathy began to paint them into her collection. The initial paintings were small (2-1/2" x 3-1/2"), predominately watercolor and ink, and with a monochromatic palette: earthy browns, beiges, taupes, grays, and greens. But even in their small size, the exuberance in the dancing, swaying limbs, the skeletal structure of the trees, and the extreme joy that exuded from each brushstroke was obvious. When she brought the finished pieces to Bartlett, she was inspired to go larger, and began experimenting with a wood-burning tool, creating a series of intricate, woodcarvings. The porous surfaces absorbed earthy wood stains, mixed with subtle streaks of acrylic green, blue and red paints, thereby enhancing the natural tree rings and knots. Here, in these carvings, the spirited faces begin to emerge.

She brought this concept to larger birch panels (12"x24"), where one face flowed into the next, creating sinuous tree limbs and collective tales of life. For the exhibition, the gallery was transformed into a forest, with each panel, whether standing alone or part of a diptych or triptych, speaking to the other, acknowledging its importance and contribution to the whole work.

I have always been in awe of trees—their wisdom, their

strength, their constant stewardship of the ground they root. I remember a little blackberry tree in front of my childhood home, picking its plump juicy berries and discovering a bird's nest inside. I felt I had to stop so that the mother bird would have enough food to feed her babies. There were more than enough berries to feed us all. Trees seem to give more fruit the more they are harvested.

Kathy shares this sacred view with me. Growing up in a wonderfully diverse neighborhood in St. Louis, Missouri, she enjoyed massive old sycamore, maple, and oak trees that were just as much a part of the community as any resident. From her front window, she would see an elderly Japanese man sitting on his front porch every morning staring and contemplating a lone tree that stood in the center of his yard, which seemed to have a connection to the center of his being. Watching her neighbors play baseball, grow all-American roses, and play percussive instruments were daily occurrences that contributed to a feeling of safety and community; everyone knew everyone else and was always there to help.

Centered around the church and its teaching of fellowship, Kathy's parents opened their home for community events to everyone in the neighborhood. Her mother believed it was important to galvanize a sense of community and show support, especially to those who could not find it elsewhere. These images and stories set the foundation for Kathy's art to embody her commitment towards community.

I created this book because I believe in the same message Kathy's art so beautifully depicts. That although we traverse various paths wearing different faces and masks, healing different wounds and scars, sharing different histories and stories, we merge by creating a unified network, a creative community, a forest of spirited trees.

As I began meeting new people, some with the intention of

writing art and sustainability features and others who just simply sprung into my life and with whom I instantly connected, I began to hear similar words. They told of where they came from, what they believed, and how they tirelessly work towards building community. These diverse yet similar people would ultimately end up being the subjects featured in this book.

I began by researching, immersing myself in different religions, mythologies, and cultures. Even though I was fascinated by all of this information – it was just that – information that seemed distant to me, removed from the now. Living in the moment is critical for living a life that encourages creativity and community. And it was in this early stage of preliminary dialogue with these local individuals that I began to see reflections of others and hear the echoes from their words.

Often we polarize ourselves by focusing on the differences, when in reality, community is about coming together and building from a passion that emerges from the center of our being. How can this be done when each person has their own vision? By reaching beyond our limits like tree branches.

Today, everyone seems to be caught in a struggle. Every day we are inundated with news of more and more violence, crisis, and chaos affecting the economy, politics, and the environment. We seem to absorb this outer turmoil which in turn creates feelings of hopelessness in ourselves. Often, when we allow greed to dictate our actions, everything around us seems to crumble.

After experiencing Spirited Trees in 2009, I became even more sensitized to world events. I felt the shattering of Haiti's earthquake, I shivered in Europe's deep freeze, I drowned in Japan's tsunami that swallowed up lives in mere seconds. And then there were those close to us who have lost their homes, their jobs, their dignity. There was so much to say and people began clamoring in the streets – in New York, in Cairo, in Tripoli and Damascus – uprisings, uproars, anger erupting. It was like watching a steaming volcano, spewing sparks, and then overflowing a paralyzing wrath. Here and there, people's emotions are swaying on extremes and the sounds are circumnavigating the globe.   These stories of catastrophic storms that have demolished cities and destroyed people's lives need to be heard in our own corner of the world. They remind us that we are part of a delicate ecosystem and that these disasters are not isolated from our own existence. They affect agriculture and food production, economy and insurance rates, human health and nature's biodiversity.

Everyone that is featured in this book has a different voice, background, and set of beliefs, but what they do have in common is their commitment to building community and sustainable living. Those lifelong intentions are the thread that connects them to each other and to you and me. We are interdependent; we are an ecosystem and society that relies on the support of our past and the spirit of the future. This is community. Our stories should be disseminated to future generations so we do not lose history, so they know we cared about them, so that they will care for others that will come after—like the eggs in the blackberry tree.

My hope for this book is that it expands your heart and moves you to act in compassion for those living in your corner of the world and those beyond your reach. That it awakens you to see everyone and everything as a part of nature; to become engaged in this coexistence rather than separated by it; that it quiets your worries, lessens your fears, and strengthens your song so that you can enjoy the silence and listen, listen, listen to the voices in Spirited Trees, which will be your own.

Kathy Hirshon Biography

Kathy Ryan Hirshon (born August 17, 1949, in St. Louis, Missouri) is an American artist and educator. Revered for her public and private mural commissions, outdoor art exhibitions and fundraisers, and group gallery presentations, Kathy has created art her whole life for the purpose of cultivating joy, communicating life's beauty, and ultimately, to share these aesthetic emotions with others. Often whimsical in nature, her work evokes delight from everyone who experiences it. In 2009, Kathy was asked to participate in the Bartlett Arboretum's plein air art auction in Stamford, which in turn launched her artwork into a new direction. Always true to her credo of creating art for enjoyment, coupled with the desire to be surrounded by beauty, nature, and symbols of self-reflection, Kathy embarked on a distinctive path that delved deeper into the myths and mysteries of life. Invigorated by a new spiritual purpose, Kathy created Spirited Trees, an acclaimed collection of work that comes alive through a seamless union of spirit and matter, as if formed from breath and dust. Her internal search of self and anima yielded a unique body of work, which also inspires the pursuit of sustainable living and creative community, and serves as a herald for global peace. Presently, Kathy travels between Stamford, Connecticut and Santa Fe, New Mexico creating art, teaching workshops, and continually expanding the Spirited Trees collection into a populated forest of visual, timeless stories.

E choes: Listening to the Voices in Spirited Trees is a collection of work that can be opened at any page; no one chapter needs to be read first to understand the next. Each section contains images of the Spirited Trees artwork, in which I begin with a poem and a question, a deep meditation of what I see in these pieces. My wish is for you, reader, to contemplate your own response, so that your voice becomes part of the poem. Following are interviews of individuals whom I feel embody the essence of each panel's message. You may decide to read each chapter in sequence as if walking side-by-side with me. Or you may choose to wander from one tree to another, creating your own journey.

ECHOES
LISTENING TO THE VOICES IN SPIRITEDTREES

Author: Michelina Docimo
Artist: Kathy Hirshon

Editor: Rosemary Serluca-Foster
Printmaker: Michael Van der Linden
Book design by ShiftFWD

BEING

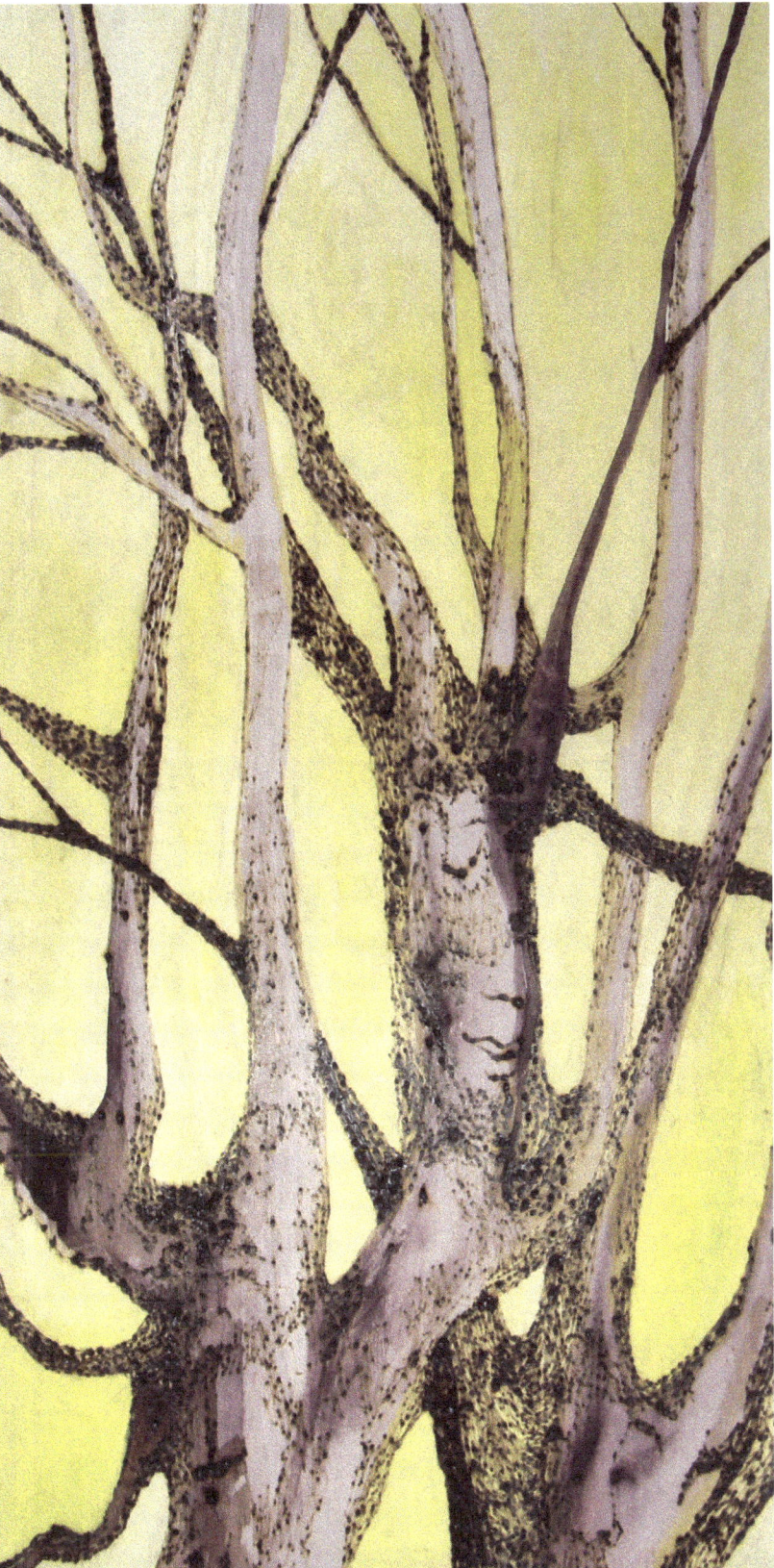

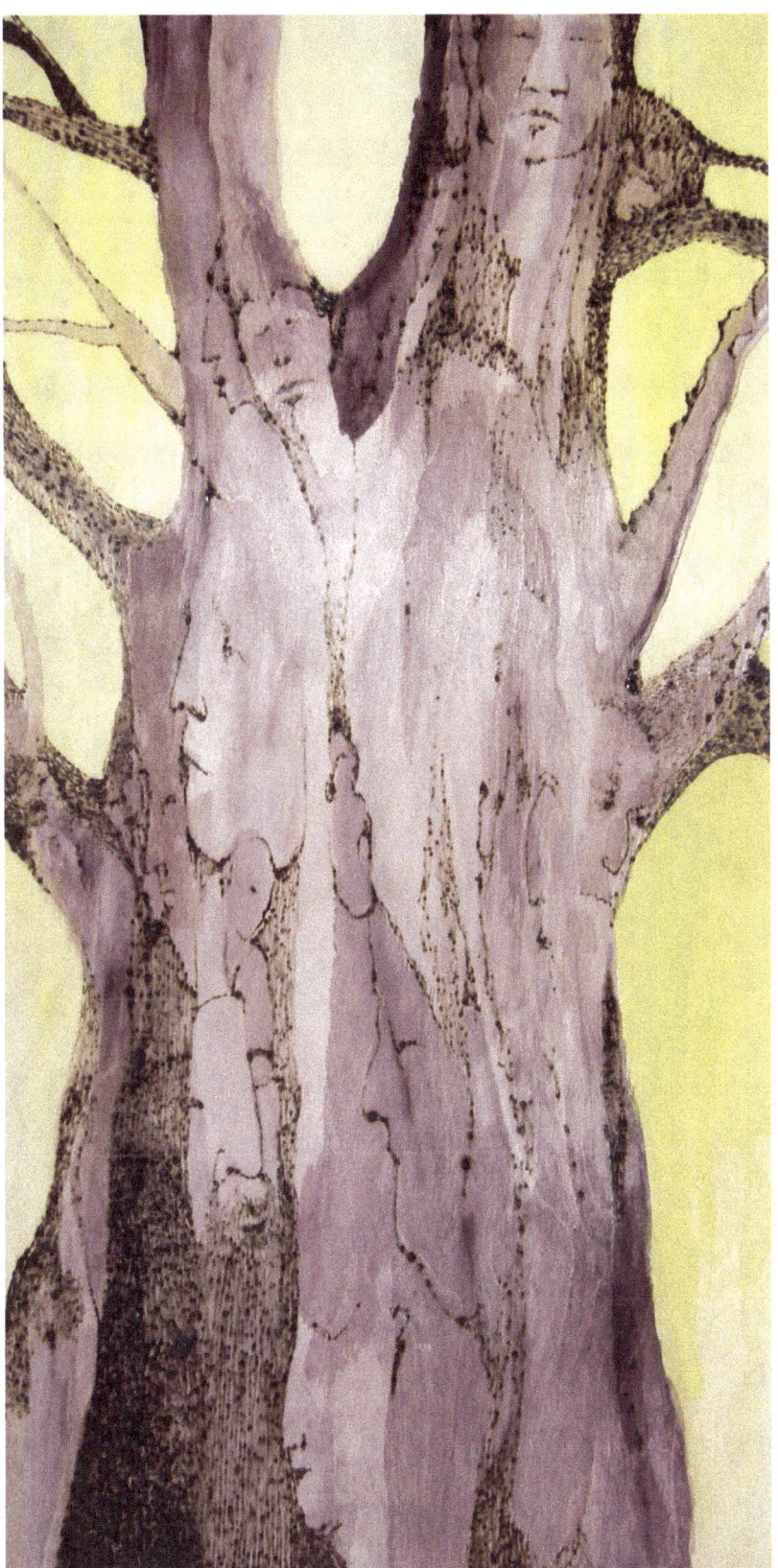

BEING

Q: When do we cease to be?
A: _____

Who are you? What is your name? Where do you come from?
We are human beings and we are spiritual beings,
With basic needs for air, water, shelter, food, fire,
And of the need for peace, justice, freedom--basic human rights.

The right to live and feed our spiritual beings,
To grow our capacity to empathize,
For from empathy grows compassion,
From compassion grows community, unfolding.

Those severed from society,
Cut from a universal soul,
Separated from nature, their capacity to empathize is lost;
Resources, symmetry, connection--lost.

In certain places and times,
In the past and in the now,
Not everyone was or is allowed to be who they really are.
Where does this leave us, if we are not allowed to be our true selves?

Being, a solid trunk strongly rooted,
Begins divergence at the center, splitting off into two limbs,
Coming together again,
Into a crown of many branches.

Air pockets connect distant relationships;
There is balance, there is symmetry.
One face bleeds into the next, purple branches basking in sunlight,
Some with eyes open, others closed, at ease in a perfect state of Being.

Moses Boone

In a world where most seems broken, promises are mere tokens from which we can further lose hope. Oaths, vows, votes, pledges, contracts, covenants, spoken words of promise have no meaning, unless, like the sun, you keep rising every morning. The future is promised to no one. Who is Moses Boone? He is someone who continues rising, someone who owns his words when he speaks of creating a brighter future. Mellow, even, bass, low, Moses' voice bellows like manly blues and then sometimes skips in a childlike singsong sound.

It is the 10th of December and I'm meeting with Moses. "Today is a national holiday in Sweden," he says, "the day when the Nobel Prizes are presented in Stockholm."

I met Moses while taking a sustainable building advisor course at Gateway Community College in North Haven, Connecticut. He sat in the back asking questions, sharing stories, his voice booming over my head. We had never directly exchanged words, until one day, passing in front of me he said, "Let me guess, you're the youngest in a family of only girls."

I was astonished. "How did you know?" I asked. "Oh, I can tell," he laughed. I figured he came from a family full of sisters.

Moses is an eco-community leader at Colored Planet, a nonprofit he founded in 2009. The organization's mission is to shed "a sun ray of hope in the New Haven region... to advocate for the creation of long lasting clean tech solutions to reduce joblessness and foster adoption of renewable energy projects in the urban environments to bridge the gap between the eco-haves and the eco-have nots." *It's a mouthful and what lingers in the air is this concept of the eco-haves and the eco-have nots and to which do we belong. People have always been categorized by age, race, gender, status, and religion. But have people ever been asked--are you eco-deprived?-- are you an eco-minority?--do you advocate for your eco-rights? Colored Planet seeks to restore spirit in the community by revitalizing a sense of responsibility for our ecology, local economy, and food and energy sources. It is an all-encompassing effort to rise every morning and face present and future challenges.

> *I existed from all eternity and, behold, I am here; and I shall exist till the end of time, for my being has no end.*
>
> *~Kahlil Gibran*

Born to Pentecostal Christian parents who were both ministers, Moses' home was full of preaching. At age eight, Moses and his family moved from New York to Virginia, where his grandparents owned a farm of mostly cash crops: peanuts, soybeans, cotton, and corn. It was the late 1950s and racism in the south was the norm, a time when color defined you, a time when the promise of being united was being separated.

Every week, Moses received an allowance for doing his chores. Today, he shares a story with me of wanting to use his allowance to treat himself to a hamburger and milkshake at a local restaurant. Innocently walking in, seating himself at the counter, ready to indulge in his appetent meal, five waitresses passed in front of him, back and forth, taking other customers' orders while ignoring him. After watching and waiting, Moses let one of the waitresses know he was ready to order.

Moses:
" 'Stand up and go to the door to place your order, boy' she drawled at me. So I did.

I got up, went to the door, placed my order, and then went back to the counter to sit down. Then she told me I couldn't eat it in the restaurant. That I had to take my meal outside. I was confused. I didn't understand why I had to eat outside. When I went home I asked my father why I had to eat my meal outside. His answer was, 'It's time for us to leave.' We moved back to Bed-Stuy in Brooklyn, New York where neighborhoods weren't only made up of Southern blacks and Southern whites. I remember Russian immigrant neighbors who taught me how to play chess and Jewish candy store clerks who would drop an extra gumball or two in my bag. I remember seeing serial numbers tattooed on their forearms.

I never asked what those numbers were for, but I remember watching television and seeing the U.S. military go into concentration camps. The bodies were stacked high. They were very dark images that will stay with me forever."

The South was not forgotten either. Moses continued to visit his grandparents' farm in Newsom, Virginia, during summer vacations. Just like me. Except my summer vacations took me to my grandparents' farm in Italy. Those were vacations that really meant something. It wasn't just a flag on a map; it was a place with a spirit. I remember sneaking into the chicken coop, picking up hens to see if they had laid any eggs. I remember making masks out of grape leaves. And I remember leaving. Those mornings were painful, full of tears, a long winding drive in tears. I couldn't speak. No matter how many times we went back, it was the leaving that made me feel empty. How many vacations did my mother give up to

* *"Colored Planet Mission Statement," last modified April 15, 2011, http://www. coloredplanet.org/mission-statement*

take care of my grandmother when she became old and sick? All of them. Those vacations meant something.

Moses' grandparents began using chemical fertilizers, fungicides on seeds, and DDT. It was the summer of 1961. Moses had finished working in the fields and decided to go fishing in the river, where he had always caught fish before. That day, nothing.

Moses:
"I caught nothing. No matter what bait I used, I caught only a few bottom feeders. Day after day, the same thing. Fishing, and there were no fish. It wasn't until several years later, after I read Rachel Carson's *Silent Spring*, that I realized the relationship between the farm runoff and how it adversely affected the ecosystem. We ruined the rivers. There was no more life in those muddy waters."

Moses shares more stories of his youth and how partying and dancing were not allowed in his father's house, only church music.

Moses:
"Attending Brooklyn College opened a new world for me. I would sneak off to jazz clubs to hear music. I fell in love with jazz and met cutting edge musicians like Dizzy Gillespie, John Coltrane, Max Roach, and Cecil Taylor, all pioneers in jazz music. I loved to dance. I spent more time dancing than studying. Then came Vietnam. For six years, I volunteered on medical evacuation missions."

As he tells me this, episodes of the TV series, MASH flash in my mind. I don't always understand war language. I don't understand the years, the politics, the governments, the places, the years; how long does war last. All the facts become mud in my head. I tune out. Not on purpose, not out of ignorance, not that it isn't history and that I don't respect the lives lost or that I don't want to learn, but I wonder how many, in generations to come, will tune out. Who will see the scars through the plumes of smoke? Do we really develop as a world through war? We keep fighting.

Moses brings me back by telling me a more personal story, a story of life and death, of his life and death, and the fine line between the two. In his late twenties, he suddenly became ill. He stopped dancing. He contracted spinal meningitis and became gravely ill.

Moses:
"I had a near death experience. I remember seeing bright lights and hearing a chorus of voices. They were telling me it was not my time. Not my time to go. I had to go back. When I came back, I realized that I always needed to choose light."

The way Moses chose light was to receive light, follow light, and give light. Back in his dancing days, Moses had met a Swedish woman in a jazz club that introduced him to a Japanese philosophy and spiritual practice called Sukyo Mahikari. (Sukyo means universal principles and Mahikari means light energy.*)

Practioners of the practice transmit positive light energy through the palms of their hands, which is said to purify and revitalize the spirit, mind and body. In this way, Moses learned to give and receive light.

He immersed himself in studying the universal principles, how all of one's actions and choices lead to spiritual growth, how one can find meaning in life's experiences. Sukyo Mahikari is a philosophy of personal and spiritual growth that encourages the sharing of joy and light with everyone.

Moses moved to Sweden where he started his family, completed his bachelors of arts in philosophy, with minors in anthropology and dance, and lived in divine light for many years. As his children became older, he thought of his own aging parents and decided to move back to the United States to care for them. He feared receiving a call one day, the voice on the other end letting him know that either his mother or father had passed. There was distance. Years of distance. And even though his father was angry, angry that Moses left the family, angry that he left the Pentecostal religion, there was also love. Moses returned home.

> *At times I feel as if I am spread out over the landscape and inside things, and am myself living in every tree, in the splashing of waves, in the clouds and the animals that come and go, in the procession of the seasons.*
>
> *~Carl Jung*

Moses:
"We've all done things in our life that we're not proud of, but you can erase these errors. You can be cleansed with divine light. I wanted to return the love my parents gave me when I could not care for myself, when I had become so ill and could not care for myself."

Moses shares the eulogy he read at his father's funeral with me. The first word is a "thanks," a thanks for caring for him and the family, for loving them, guiding them, for being a father. Moses opened his heart to his family and friends that day, to all the people of the many congregations that his father had shepherded as a pastor. He recalled the trips back and forth, north and south, which always led him back home, to his family. Time is never enough when you are with the ones you love.

Carrying out his filial duties, Moses bade farewell to his father with open arms, just as his father had received him. But it did not end with words. Moses continues to act as a caretaker for his mother, he continues to lead advocacy groups on issues of sustainability, he continues to teach people how to grow their own food and how to rely on each other for maintaining a strong community. Moses keeps his promises.

The sun is setting. The sky becomes streaked with sienna and plum. As the December afternoon slips away, the last glimpse of light falls on to Moses' face. He shares that when it is his time to leave this earth, he wants his ashes buried under the Sequoia trees, the oldest living trees on the planet. He tells me all this with a note of anticipation. He remembers the persimmon tree on his grandparents' farm, a single tree in the middle of a field, and how as a little boy he would climb it and listen to the birds' songs.

*"Sukyo Mahikari .", www.sukyomahikari.org

TENDING

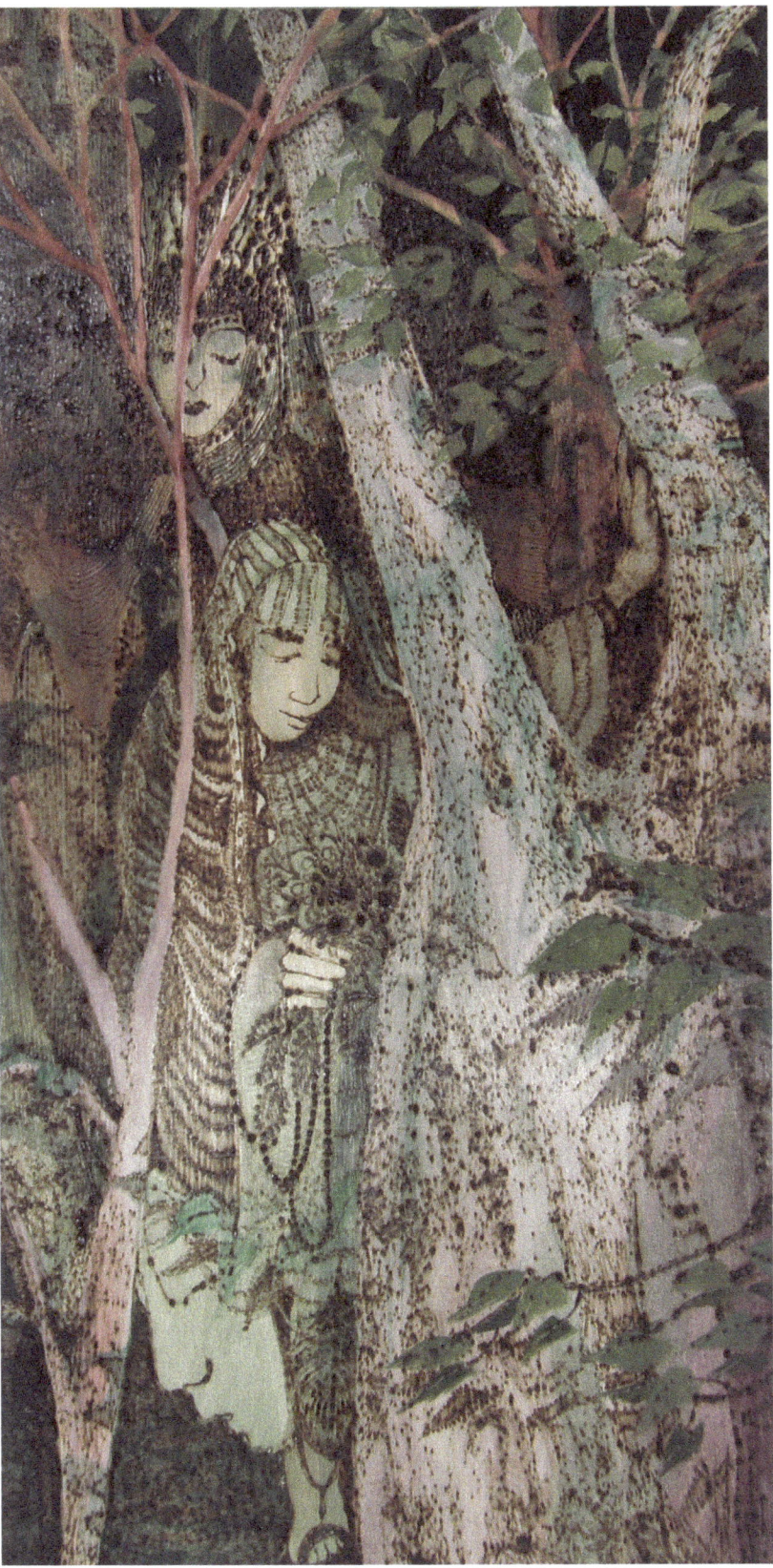

TENDING

Q: How do you nurture your garden?
A: _____

Destruction, drought, famine, pain,
Homelessness, hunger, poverty, waste
For many--social, cultural, environmental truths
In their inner and outer gardens.

Some see such ills as separate from life,
Beyond mend, repair, outside their world
Sister, brother, stranger--in despair right next door
Poor communities can't help themselves; gardens grown wild,
broaden.

Amongst the trees, well-groomed faces emerge from Tending,
A child and its mother look back in,
To a lush green forest, their glances cast down,
Mother upon child, child upon tree, tree upon soil.

A lineal connection, a native understanding,
Of the ancient and natural order of life
Tending, reaping, sowing, tending, reaping, sowing,
We inherit the earth and each other.

Wearing a crown-like headdress,
Mother offers nurturing power,
Her guiding hands grace ancient trees,
Teaching the reverence of family and nature.

Wearing shawl and sandals,
Cupping prayer beads and flowers,
The child learns the substance of stewardship,
His earthly and spiritual gardens, never depleted, never barren.

Laura DePreta

"We're all born," Laura begins, "this is what we have in common. Everyone on this earth is born and then everyone will die. We were born to die."

Laura and I laugh as she says this because it is so simple, so true, frightfully, funnily true. My mother says this, my grandmothers used to say this, and I am certain my great-grandmothers also said, "We are all born to die." The teapot whistles, blowing a steady stream of steam into the air. Laura pours me a cup of tea over a teaspoon of honey.

Laura and I have much in common; we are both avid gardeners. Several years ago, we met at the Bartlett Arboretum in Stamford where she was to lead a volunteer group in establishing the first herb garden on the arboretum's grounds. The group was supposed to dig ground and lay bricks for pathways. Laura and I were the only two that showed up that day. It was hard work, physical work, rewarding work. That was how we met, laying bricks for walkways in a garden.

While planting thyme, nasturtiums, marshmallow, and a mélange of other culinary, medicinal, and fragrant herbs, I remember Laura talking about delivering babies--her babies, her sister's babies, her clients' babies. She was so open with sharing intimate details about giving birth. This is Laura—open, honest, and filled with creative energy. She enjoys keeping a beehive, growing a vegetable garden, and raising chickens in her backyard. But what she loves most is teaching expectant mothers and fathers about childbirth, a process, she believes, is the most creative act we can participate in.

I previously wrote about Laura's childbirth classes and the connection between giving birth and living green on April 26, 2010, for *Connecticut Green Scene*, a blog about sustainable living. She shared that giving birth naturally is an ancient art, but that it may now be in danger of becoming a lost one. In the United States, Cesarean sections are at an all-time high, a procedure that forces women to become disconnected from their bodies, the breathing, the pushing, and ultimately, the baby. Why is this? Have we become lazy? Are we evolving into a creatively lazy society?

I believe that Laura's passion for educating couples about natural childbirth is critical in beginning a healthy life, so today I find myself in her presence once again, this time, in her glowing, Tuscan kitchen. "Everything is about convenience now, everything, even childbirth," says Laura. "Having a child is hard work, it is not easy work. But raising a child is even more work. The woman's physical labor has been removed and replaced with quick and convenient C-sections, often so the doctor can avoid being held liable if something were to go wrong. Today, we deliver babies the same way we deliver fast food--fast."

In Italian, "dare la luce" means to give light and is used to allude to the act of a woman giving birth. Natural childbirth or "giving light" is a concept that may seem foreign to many, one that is often replaced with a delivery process that takes place from behind closed doors in cold, steely gray, and windowless rooms. Laura, who is a Bradley Method trained childbirth educator and co-founder of Informed Beginnings, is shedding light on childbirth options through classes on pre- and postnatal nutrition, partner support coaching, comfort and relaxation measures during labor, and what to expect after delivery. Informed Beginnings is a co-op of instructors from all over the country who teach evidence-based childbirth classes, revealing the balance between the art and science of twenty-first century birthing. She empowers pregnant women and their partners by helping them to make educated decisions on the best way to bring forth a new life into the world.

What's so green about giving birth to a baby naturally? Everything. It's about taking responsibility and making healthy decisions for yourself and your family. As a society, we have become so detached from nature that we have even lost sight of something so primal as giving birth, something women's bodies are made to do naturally.

In the late 80s, Laura was young, unwed, and pregnant. Fortunately, she discovered the Maternity Center Association on the upper east side of Manhattan. It was here that she fell in love with her independence as a woman. The center allowed women to be a part of every aspect of the birthing process, even before the physical labor began. Laura recalls measuring her own weight, recording her own urine analysis, and reading her own charts, all under the guidance of trained midwives. The emotional support from her boyfriend at the time was peripheral; physically present, but also in the dark as to what to do or expect. The center provided the emotional support she was not able to get from other places.

A self-proclaimed quitter, Laura quickly realized you cannot give up when giving birth. "I learned to understand what was happening to my body, what stage I was in, how to surpass the next level of pain, and how to keep going until I reached the release of a new life. Giving birth is exhilarating, our bodies heal, and a natural amnesia occurs that allows you to forget the pain."

Each of her three childbirths differed in time and intensity. For her third child, Laura trained in the Bradley Method, which gave her the comfort of delivering in her own home, with her husband as coach, and a midwife prepared with oxygen and other equipment. Her daughter was born within three hours. I too am the third born in my family and every year on my birthday, my mother tells me the story of how quickly I was born--less than an hour.

There are many childbirth training classes available, Lamaze being one of the most well-known. What makes the Bradley Method different from the others is the focus it places on the father as a coach.

"It is imperative to create a safe place to give birth," Laura emphasizes. "When you are in such profound pain, you feel anything but safe. You go through the preparation and you work out a birth plan, but in those critical moments, you want guidance and reassurance from your partner that you will get through this. "

Laura's child birthing classes offer the expecting couple a thorough education so they can become well-informed medical consumers who understand the pros and cons at every stage: following a protein-rich diet, practicing effective birth exercises, recognizing the stages of labor, learning when and if to use an epidural, knowing when a true emergency arises requiring surgical birth, and understanding the importance of ample recovery time.

As with many journeys, the road traveled is just as important, if not more so than the destination. Childbirth is an emotional, chemical, and physical process happening inside a woman's body. The feel-good hormone oxytocin is released as the baby passes through the birth canal, promoting an indescribable love bond between mother and child.

Laura:
"About two years ago, I met up with an old friend in Miami.

Rona and I have been friends since our early twenties, when we both worked in New York. We are so different: She is an Orthodox Jew, and I, well, let's just say I have always been so natural. But we became good friends and were pregnant with our

firsts around the same time. She moved to Israel with her husband, who was a medical student and would be working within the socialized medical system there. I would share these wonderful experiences I was having at the birth center, but for her, the opposite; every one of her doctor's visits was a cold routine. Even though she was married to a doctor, she felt detached from the process. So here we were, reunited in Miami. I was with my daughters on the beach and she begins to tell them how much I influenced her into have a natural birth. I had no idea that what I had shared so long ago had made such a strong impact, how she found a connection back to her body. This was her first child and she went on to have five after that, all naturally. She thanked me on the beach that day, in front of my daughters, and it really touched me that I had a part in helping her to enjoy giving birth naturally. She also shared that during one of the births, something felt very different than the others and she sensed something was wrong. After she delivered, her husband closed the door and let her know the baby was still born; its heart had not fully developed. Rona accepted this. After all the months of waiting and preparing, hours of labor and pain, she accepted the mystery of life. Our culture has taught us to numb pain, both physically and psychologically. When we numb labor contractions, we interfere with the physiological and emotional processes of giving birth. If a woman listens to the messages her body is sending, and she merges with this

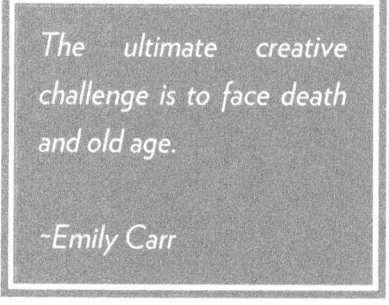

The ultimate creative challenge is to face death and old age.

~Emily Carr

process instead of fearing it, she will transcend as a human being in a way that she has never been able to do before."

Something is lost when we no longer witness how nature works. Understanding natural birthing options restores innate confidence in our bodies, each other, and nature. This illumination may lead to greener parenting methods as well, especially when it comes to decisions about a child's health.

Laura was raised in Flushing Queens, New York. Even though she lived in a concrete city, she had many opportunities to come into contact with nature. Her mother was infusing green parenting without realizing it. "My mother would take me for walks in the park. The streets in the neighborhoods were all named after trees: Ash, Beech, and Maple. My mother was so interested in trees and plants and wanted to learn the names of all of them."

We learn so much from our parents, our mothers. I grew up in a boxy house on a square block and in the center of the tiniest of front yards was an enormous pine tree. It was enormous to me when I was young because the front yard was so small and so was I. It was smack in the center, planted by my grandmother when she moved here from Italy. It was one of the first things she did to make her mark and establish new roots. My grandmother planted a pine tree in the front and my grandfather planted grape vines in the back.

"When I moved to my first place in California," Laura says, "I had an actual house and planted a garden. The property had poor soil and could barely grow anything, but my neighbor brought me a barrel of compost so that I could begin growing my garden. I became hooked!"

What a thoughtful gift. This was Laura's first experience gardening and she was already hooked. When it was time to move to the east coast, Laura's main criterion for finding a new home was that there be space for a garden. Her father would save seeds for her so that she could try growing different vegetables, like radishes, okra, and rhubarb.

Laura:

"I taught my kids to respect nature just the way my parents taught me and to not take for granted that it will always be a part of their lives. I remember when they would run up our trees when they were little. They fell asleep in those trees and when I would call for them to come down, they would go up farther! They loved those trees and would stay up there for hours. Now I realize, it's the little things I do every day that make a difference. I buy local produce through a CSA (Community Supported Agriculture); I take time to make meals; I think about what I buy, where it comes from, and the materials used to make it. I taught my children to respect nature and to see its beauty everywhere, and to take time and notice the environment around them, just like my mother taught me. These are things that are so simple to do, things that I can do with my own hands. And so can they."

So simple. I was raised between gardens too, vegetable gardens. There were always tomatoes on the vine, open squash flowers in the morning, and flaming hot peppers dangling in the garden that would make their way over doorways. All this and more grew in slim beds that lined the property, but there was always so much to share. Growing a garden was a family affair and even when we moved to a new home, we shared seeds. Seeds are thoughtful gifts. After my grandfather passed away, I remember tying packets of seeds together to give to my grandmother so she would go back in the garden, in the sunlight. It did not help. She was stubborn, but even more so, sad. She stayed inside mostly, reciting the rosary every day. "I am waiting for my day to be collected," she would say. Like a pumpkin. I could tell her time was nearing because she became more distant. It was Mother's Day and we were having dinner together. Her behavior was different, confused, rambling about people and events from the distant past mixed with those of the present. When I walked through the door, she wished me a happy Mother's Day. I smiled and said, "But I'm not a mother yet." Completely in her senses she replied, "But you're getting your nest ready."

Throughout the afternoon, I, and everyone else at the table, accepted all of her wishes: Happy Birthday, Happy Father's Day, Happy Easter. When phone calls started coming in, she wished the unsuspecting callers: Happy New Year, Merry Christmas, Happy Thanksgiving. That evening, we took her to the hospital even though she vehemently protested. She wanted to remain in the comfort of her home and every day she was away from it and in the hospital, she begged to be brought back. "I'm ready to go home," she would say. She waited and waited and finally when we told her we would be bringing her home, complete elation. As she passed through the doorway, she released a laugh so joyful, we felt a hole of hope, but that evening, her breathing became labored. Each hour became strenuous. It was happening so quickly, but it felt so slow. She was exactly where she wanted to be, at home, surrounded by her family. As we sat by her side, I could see her giving life to her spirit, setting it free into the air. What a gift she gave us to watch her go in peace, exemplifying the phrase "we are born to die." Living purposefully, respecting nature around and within, honoring life from birth until death. Being born and facing death unites us on a spiritual path. We are mere wayfarers here, wayfarers planting seeds. Every word we speak, every act we make, we breathe, plant seeds, and create life.

Emilio Funicella

About two years ago, I met Emilio Funicella, a man of a strong mind and stronger heart. Emilio had come to speak to The Flock, an adult volunteer group that met every month at The Basilica of St. John the Evangelist's rectory in Stamford, Connecticut. Before the meeting began, I noticed Emilio sitting alone in the corner, a serene but serious expression on his face, his doe-eyed King Charles Cavalier spaniel on his lap sniffing the air.

As we settled into our seats, Emilio made his way to the center of our semi-circle and began speaking to us about volunteer opportunities in the city and in the community to beautify the streets, clean the neighborhoods, create gardens, and plant trees. But not just to plant trees for the sake of planting trees. This was planting trees to make people happy.

Emilio spoke with a wide smile, his voice sometimes low, and when hitting an important point, he would get louder, repeating what he had just said to make sure we really got it. Every day he walked the streets, picking up people, people to help him plant trees. These were not ordinary people. They were men who were convicted criminals, murderers, rapists, thieves, and drug dealers. The lowest of the low. Picking them up to plant trees.

Emilio has street smarts. He knows what he knows and knows how to get things done.

Emilio:
"Last year I received an award. Can you believe it? They actually gave me an award. I received an award for what I do. What do I do? Well, I'm going to tell you what I do

with a story. A true story. The same true story I told the audience that night because I didn't have a speech prepared. So last year, I received a call from Bank of America telling me I was nominated for a Community Service Award and that the winner would receive $200,000 in grant money. Nonprofits, foundations, and established organizations were all nominated. And then there was me. I'm not in politics. I'm not an organization. I'm one guy. A private guy. So I show up to the Palace Theater in Stamford, wearing my suit and tie, and everyone else had prepared a speech. When my name was called as the winner they said all these other things right after it. All this cliché community organizer stuff. I thanked everyone and said that the only way I can explain what I do is by sharing a true story. So I told them this true story: It was two years ago, end of August. I was with a couple guys from Liberation House planting trees at Cummings Park. For those of you who don't know, Liberation House is a place dedicated to helping men rehabilitate their lives. These men can be alcoholics, drug addicts, convicted criminals, it doesn't matter, they have a place, a home, somewhere to go to so they can become whole and healthy. So, we were in Cummings Park. It was a beautiful summer day. We worked hard, enjoyed our sandwiches under the oak trees and then continued to work some more. After we were done planting trees, we piled up in the van so I could drive these guys back to Lib House. Now Billie, who is eighteen and has been to jail for drug dealing, hardly speaks. I barely hear him say two words when we're together. But that day in the van, Billie says, 'Did you see that woman that came up to me? That woman came up to me and thanked me for saving her life today. She was standing there the whole time watching us while we were working.'
What? Billie, what are you talking about? What did you say? Repeat what you said Billie. And he repeated, 'She thanked me for saving her life today.' She thanked you for saving her life today? Is it possible that we saved this woman's life

today? Is it possible? The guys asked, 'What do you mean?' I said, is it possible that we saved this woman's life today? Remember the prayer: Oh dear Lord, I do not know how long I shall live. But while I live, please let me help my fellow man with a smile, a kind word, or a good deed. Amen. How many times have I explained to you that what we do can affect the lives and hearts of another human being. What were we doing? 'We were planting trees,' the guys answered. Yes, we were planting trees. Were we having fun? 'Yeah,' they answered.

By the very act of planting trees, we are planting hope. People with no hope don't plant trees. We possibly turned her life from a state of despair into one of hope. Is that possible? Yes, of course it's possible. We saved her life today. So that's what we do. Thank you very much ladies and gentlemen."

> *Too often we under estimate the power of a touch, a smile, a kind word, a listening ear, an honest compliment, or the smallest act of caring, all of which have the potential to turn a life around.*
>
> *~Leo Buscaglia*

The rectory room was silent, and I imagine so was the Palace Theater that night.

"So, who wants to plant some trees?" Emilio let out in a raspy laugh.

The Flock went on to plant trees with Emilio and then we all went on with our individual lives. We planted trees once. Just once.

Almost a year later, I call Emilio. "I'm writing a book and I'd like to talk to you, Emilio. It's a book about trees."

"OK," he said, "come talk to me."

When I arrive at Emilio's home, he is preparing a pot of coffee. He places a dish of cookies and specialty dried figs on the table; the figs stare back at me. When the coffee is ready, he picks up the plate of sweets and says, "Let's go to my office."

Warm and wood-paneled, Emilio's office is well-stocked with books, family photographs, leather couches, and personal accessories. His three spaniels lead the way like soldiers. As we relax on to the couches, Sammy and Santana snuggle under Emilio's feet and peacefully doze off . Carter, curls up behind Emilio's ears, attentive. Lighting a cigarette, Emilio shares that he is a vice president of a major bank, but that most of his days are spent on the streets of Stamford. Planting trees. He's in his early sixties and is living a good life.

I learn that Emilio's family is from the same town that my parents are from: A small town called Rose situated in the Calabria region of southern Italy. We share roots.

Emilio begins by telling me the same story he had previously shared at the rectory, the same story he had previously shared at the Palace Theater. I don't stop him. I let him tell it again. But this time, I hear something new.

"This is what we do," he says, "it's a conversion of death to life. We dig up the ground of desolate places, we do prep work, and then we plant."

About five years ago and shortly after he began taking his Catholic faith seriously, Emilio started working with people. For most of his life, he was a non-practicing Catholic. Was he a good person? Perhaps. A person can appear outwardly good but inside there can be pain and suffering.

Emilio:

"It's a good thing to feel this pain, to be shaken to the core. This is God's work. Only through traumatic life experience can we see the depths of how we have polluted our souls, as well as all the gifts God has given us. This is good. How can I help others you ask, who are so deeply troubled? Why would I even want to? I began examining my own soul and by immersing myself in my faith, reading theology, the Bible, and the lives of saints, I discovered my inner workings. I like doing this work because it demands I live a good life. Not everyone can have contact with criminals and see the good in them. But if I can help just a little bit, just this much," (he squeezes his index and thumb together), "then I've helped convert death to life by turning their souls around. Gardening is the perfect metaphor. It teaches us patience. Peace is a very abstract term. Abstract stuff doesn't exist for me. But action is real. Every day, we can choose to nurture ourselves and the people around us, or destroy. That's it. That's the peace I like, the one that I can feel in my soul. It's about this." (Emilio points to his heart.)

I didn't have to ask many questions of Emilio; he freely opened his heart.

Emilio:

"OK, I'll tell you another story. By the way, these are all true stories. I was working with a man in his late thirties, who had spent seventeen years in jail for armed robbery. But he had gotten away with murder, literally. He had attempted to kill someone, seeking revenge for the bullet that left his brother paralyzed. This is illness of the heart. But God's mercy is greater than justice and this man was spared and started to make real inroads. He was turning his life around. A few years later, I was driving some guys back home and I heard someone screaming my name, 'Emilio, Emilio, Emilio, wait!'

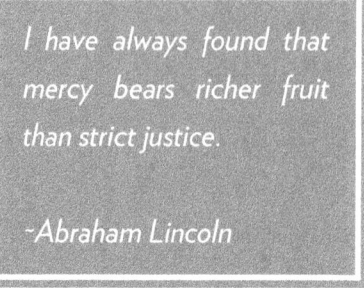

I have always found that mercy bears richer fruit than strict justice.

-Abraham Lincoln

I look in my rear view mirror and I see this guy running down the street toward my car. He reached my window, breathless, and says, 'I recognized the van, Emilio. Emilio, do you remember me? I listened to everything you said and I've never been happier in my life.' Moments like this change my life, just as much as these men believe I've helped to change theirs. Sometimes God allows evil to enter our lives as part of a purification process. If we listen, suffering can bring us closer to grace. Evil can intensify the good that comes out of this process, if we abandon ourselves to God's will. Every morning I pray, Lord, let your will be done. Everyone has emotional and material needs. But it's easy to help with those types of needs. We can make donations, send food to soup kitchens, buy toys and clothes for children, and build homes for the homeless. And still, everyone worries if they have enough, whether they are living on the streets or in a mansion. If we put our emotional needs before our material ones, we don't have to worry. Read Luke, 12:13-21 and you'll know what I'm talking about."

Chapter 12 of Luke's Gospel speaks of our earthly worries, fears, anxieties, and obsessions over our possessions. It speaks of a parable of a rich man, a rich man who brought forth plentiful fruit from the ground. Not knowing what to do with all this abundance of fruit, he builds a bigger storage barn to store his fruit away. Then he says to his soul, "Soul, thou has produced much good for many years, take thine ease, eat, drink, and be merry."*

But God calls him a fool and that very night takes away his soul. So even though he has saved treasures for himself, he is not able to enjoy the fruits of his labor because he dies. We are not rewarded by the material goods we accumulate over a lifetime; we are rewarded for our love of God and of our fellowman.

Emilio:
"Back in Italy, people starved during the wars. But even though people didn't have food, the community took care of them. People with fruit trees would allow others on to their land so everyone could gather and eat. My grandmother, Cecita, used to tell me, 'Your mother Flora is a good woman.' And then she would tell me how when these starving people would come by the house, they would ask whoever happened to be home if they could pick fruits. When my Aunt Elvira was home, she would tell them, 'Yes, but only take six.' But when my mother was home, she would say, 'Take as much as you want.'
The poor people would then say to my grandmother, 'When we come to your home, Elvira tells us we can take only six pieces of fruit, but when Flora is there, she tells us we can take as much as we want.' My grandmother was a wise woman and didn't take sides. She just said, 'Come when Flora is home. Come when Flora is home.' "

One story leads to another, and then another, and then another, and before we know it, three hours have passed. Having traveled back to a time when Emilio and I did not even exist. But still, he knows the stories so well, as if he had been there himself.

As I prepare to leave, Emilio makes his way to a bookshelf, pulls out a book and hands it to me: *I Believe in Love.* "I love this book, he says, "it's based on the teaching of St. Therese of Lisieux. You should read it. I think you'll like it. Keep it."
I pack my notes and he adds, almost disappointed, "You didn't eat anything."

I thank him for our time together and let him know that I too am familiar with these fig treats; my grandmother made them.

I remember receiving packages of dried figs stuffed with walnuts from her at Christmastime. She would send them packed with orange leaves. They always reminded me of four leaf clovers or daisies or butterflies, but as I say the word "crucetti" to Emilio, and having listened to his stories of faith, I realize they are little crosses. I always knew the word meant little crosses, but at that moment, after listening to Emilio's stories and perspective on faith, the meaning became clearer.

"Someone just came from Italy and brought them to me. You take them," Emilio insists. I want him to savor them and say, "No, enjoy them Emilio." But instead he slides the figs into a zip lock bag, hands it to me and says, "No, you enjoy them."

Sometimes driving around Stamford, I see Emilio doing what he does best, working, cleaning, pruning, planting, and now I know what he is really doing – saving lives, planting hope.

*Luke, 12:13-21, Parable of the Rich Fool

SEEKING SUSTENANCE

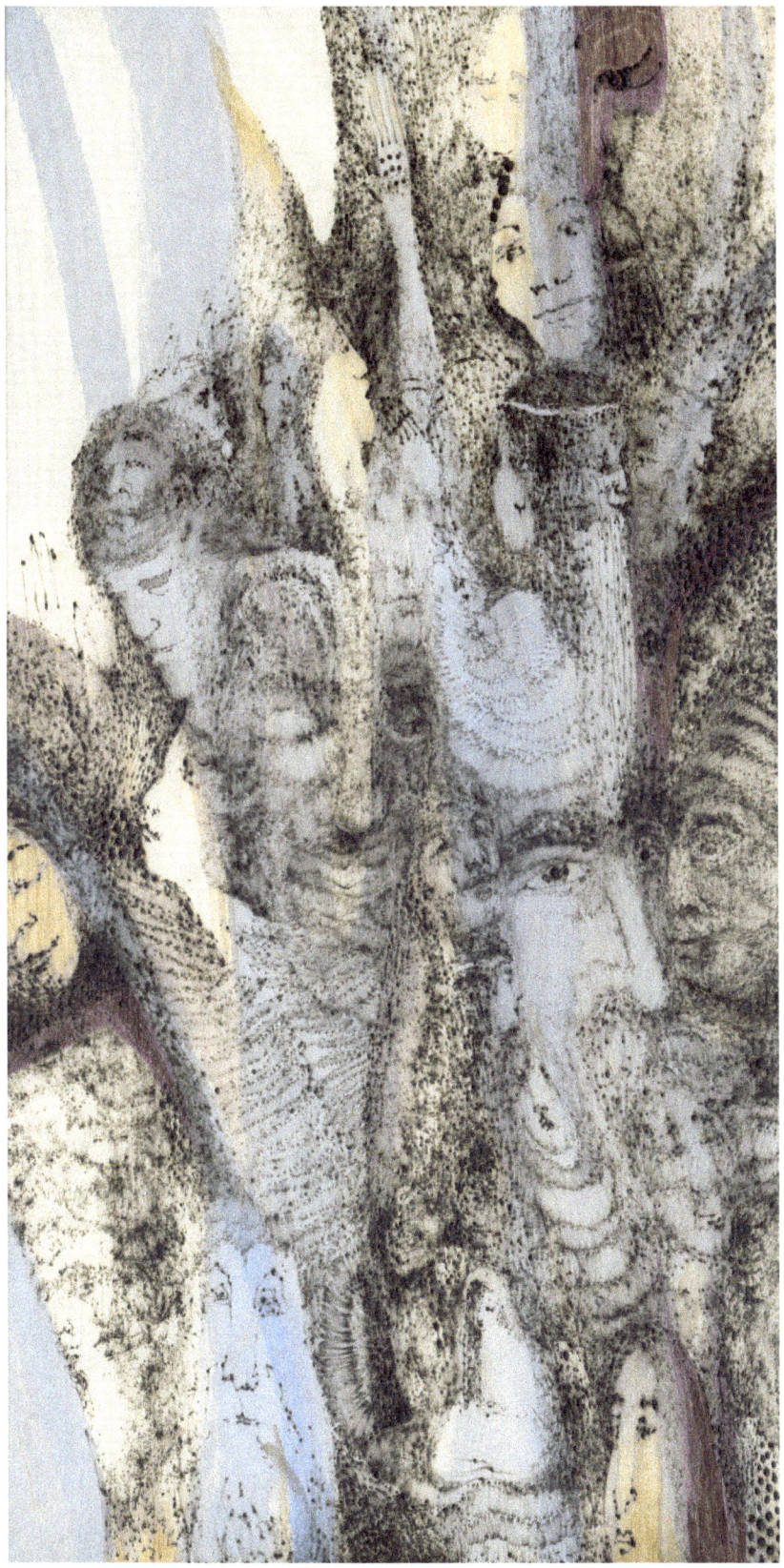

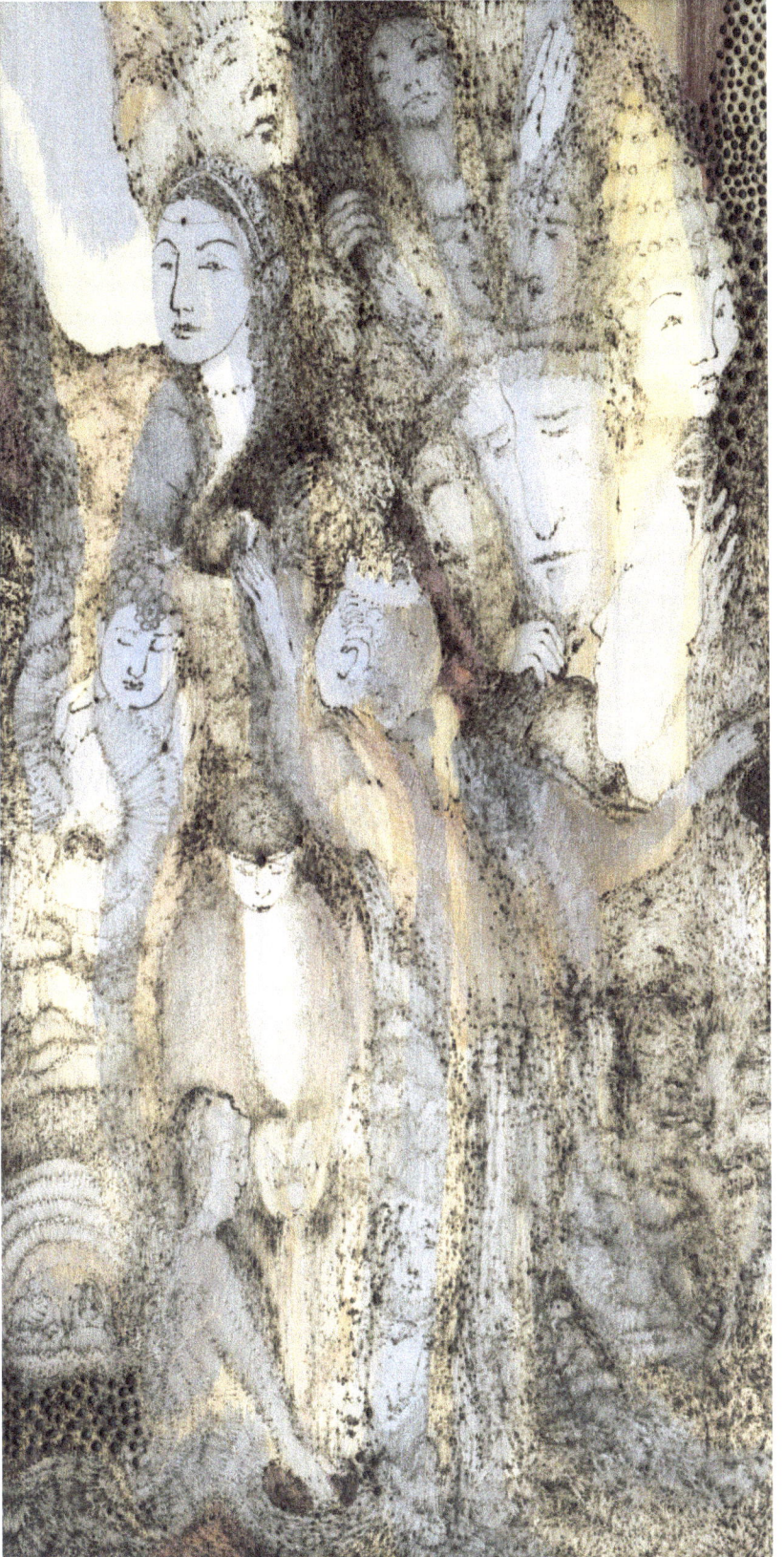

SEEKING SUSTENANCE

Q: How will we survive?
A: _____

Hungry for power, powered by ego,
In a land flowing with milk and honey
We walk through life eating apples,
Feeling empty, feeling lost.

We search for more nourishment,
To fill bodies and minds
These pangs grow strong,
As we swallow the lies.

Our mouths become parched,
Unable to speak the truth
We are choked, we are voiceless,
As we swallow our tears.

Hollow, we start to see inside,
Through crumbled walls and shattered glass
A space made wide
From fertile soil and flowing water; an oasis for spirit.

Cascades of hungry faces pour into each other,
Like waterfalls, they grasp at pieces of wisdom
Seeking Sustenance to find a feast,
Like a child at its mother's bosom.

Inhaling the scent of earth and bread,
We satisfy the spirit with a grain of wheat
A drop of dew, a strand of pearls
Collecting quietly in a bowl; we are hungry, like wolves.

Selma Miriam & Noel Furie

About five years ago, a friend was de-cluttering his home and clearing his shelves of books he no longer wanted. "I thought you would like these," he said, as he graciously handed me three old books from the 1970s that had belonged to his mother: Peck: cento anni, 1883-1983*, which is a cookbook written in Italian, Better Homes and Gardens New Garden Book†, and The Political Palate: A Feminist Vegetarian Cookbook.+

I thanked him, scanned through the yellowed pages and decided the books were definitely worth keeping. Peck: cento anni and Better Homes and Gardens made their way to my bookshelf, but The Political Palate got lost in the shuffle. I searched for months but could not find it anywhere. I considered it missing and put it out of mind.

In November 2009, soon after my review of Kathy Hirshon's Spirited Trees was published in *ARTES Magazine*, I was inspired to continue writing pieces that focused on nature and green art. Selma Miriam, a masterful weaver and expert at using natural dyes in textile arts was recommended as a potential feature piece.

Selma is a very busy woman. In addition to her weaving artistry, she runs Bloodroot—a vegan and vegetarian restaurant/feminist bookstore—on the water's edge in Bridgeport, Connecticut.

*I Fratelli Stopani, Peck: cento anni, 1883-1983 (Milano, Librex S.p.A, 1983)

† Better Homes and Gardens New Garden Book (Des Moines, Meredith Publishing Company, 1961).

+The Bloodroot Collective, The Political Palate: A Feminist Vegetarian Cookbook (Bridgeport, Sanguinaria Publishing, 1980).

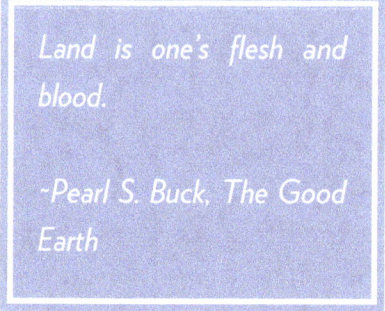

Land is one's flesh and blood.

-Pearl S. Buck, The Good Earth

I met Selma at her home on a misty fall day in November of 2010. Crimson maple leaves carpeted the walkway to her front door, bolstering the dreary gray sky above. Selma opened the door wearing blue jean overalls, her white hair pulled back into a long braid that swung over her shoulder. As I entered her home, I felt as if I was gliding into a different time, a time when things were simpler and slower.

Three wooden spinning wheels sat still and silent, while the walls, embellished in woven art and lace, whispered welcome. Selma and I moved into the kitchen where she sat at the head of the table, a pot of indigo dye between her feet. "Indigo is an amazing dye," she said. "The plant parts need to be in an alkaline solution which is a clear liquid. When you add fabric into the liquid, it remains white. And then, as you pull it out, the oxygen in the air reacts to create the blue color." Selma dipped the fabric in and out of the bucket several times demonstrating the chemical process. "It's like magic."

Dripping, handmade fibers hung like patches of blue sky on a clothesline from the back porch to the end of the property line. Annexed to the kitchen was a greenhouse swarming with an array of orchid varieties. Selma talked about her younger days as a landscape designer and how she traveled to South American jungles to study orchids. Even though she has a great love for nature and design, she began despising the unnatural economics of the business. She left it behind to pursue her dream—a vegetarian restaurant/bookstore. Her vision crystallized when she opened Bloodroot in 1977. As Selma shared this with me, I immediately realized she was the author of The Political Palate. "I have your book!" I said, excited to have made the connection. I did not have the heart to let her know it was lost.

Selma walked me through the rest of her home presenting colorful winter hats, soft wool socks, intricately threaded linens, and triangular tasseled shawls, all made by her hands. Lace treatments covered the French-trimmed windows and a quilt featuring Isis, the Egyptian goddess of magic and life, draped gracefully from the ceiling. All of this artistic handiwork on display in her home has never been on display in a museum or studio. To Selma, her art is her life, whether in private or in public.

I wrote the piece about Selma and her many creative talents, but it did not get published. A year later, when I was deciding who to feature in the Spirited Trees book, Selma immediately came to mind.

It's November again, but this time it is a spectacularly sunny day. Selma has invited me to meet her at Bloodroot. I step out of my car into the restaurant's empty parking lot. The shimmering water and salty air makes me miss summer. Bloodroot looks and feels like a cottage with its flagstone outdoor patio adjacent to a mature cherry tree and herb garden bed, which is preparing for deep winter rest. A woman with large-framed glasses answers the door and lets me in. She introduces herself as Noel, tells me to help myself to a table, Selma will be right out.

I sit and take in the walls covered with textile art and vintage photos, the mismatched wooden tables and chairs, and the familiar form of an old-fashioned but completely functioning spinning wheel. The semi-open kitchen allows guests visual access to food preparation and cooking, but all of that activity has yet to begin today. Towards the back and up two steps are bookshelves filled with feminist theory publications, political paperbacks, and nature novels, plus wingback armchairs so old and comfy, you may never get up once you have settled in.

Selma walks out of the kitchen with an air of agility, her white braid still over her shoulder. As we sit down, Bella, the restaurant cat, slinks onto my lap so I can pet her silky coat. Selma shares the good news that Yale University's Sterling Memorial Library recently acquired the Bloodroot Collective Records.*

Four, 3 X 4 storage boxes containing letters, posters, photos, advertisements, news clippings, financial records, correspondence from famous feminist writers like Adrienne Rich and Audre Lorde, and many other creative works have been fortunately preserved for future generations. I can tell from Selma's demeanor that she is proud of this recognition and shares the honor by telling me it was a collaborative effort by all of the women who have worked for Bloodroot over the years.

Noel walks over and joins us at the table.

"Did you meet Noel?" Selma asks. "She is my partner."

Noel and I are attentive as Selma continues to share more of Bloodroot's rich history.

In 1977, Selma wanted to create a woman's center that would serve nutritious food for the mind and body. Its purpose would be to further the feminist movement. Selma noticed back then that even though it was traditional for women to be in their own kitchens at home, it was rare, if not impossible, to find a woman restaurateur and even more rare for the public to see women working together. It was also virtually impossible for women to secure funding for a new business. With a loan from Fay Davidson, her suffragist mother, Selma purchased the waterfront property and realized that anything is possible.

Bloodroot, named after a self-sowing native wildflower, is more than a meeting place, more than a restaurant, more than a bookstore. It is a place of eclectic thought that has attracted a multifarious mix of musicians, politicians, speakers, artists, and poets—all of them unique thinkers.

Selma:

"I feel it is important to live a moral life. 'What is a moral life?' some may ask. If you truly want to live a moral life, everything you do, everything you eat, everything you wear, everything you buy must be selected in a way that considers whether or not the action respects the spirit of Mother Nature. The restaurant is vegetarian because we see a correlation between the abuse and slaughter of animals and the exploitation of women. These feminist ideas may seem antiquated now because much progress has been made for women's rights, but in the 1970s, women were still regarded as lesser beings. We have made strides in bringing women together who were hungry for more than a meal; they were hungry to be heard. This restaurant is open to all; in fact many men come to eat here because the food is delicious. Our healthy produce is purchased from local farmers and CSAs (Community Supported Agriculture). We also tend to our own smaller gardens on the property and utilize in-season, organic fruits and vegetables to create our meals. Bloodroot is a different experience in many ways—as soon as you enter, you serve yourself. "

Everybody needs beauty as well as bread, places to play in and pray in, where nature may heal and give strength to body and soul.

–John Muir

A young couple walks through the door with boxes loaded with fall vegetables and carries them into the kitchen. Selma tells me they are local farmers from Urban Oaks in New Britain, Connecticut, one of the best CSAs in the area. It is refreshing to see the bounty from young hands nurturing the earth worked by mature hands producing nutritious meals. Both are slow, age-old processes that connect earth to people, to more people, and more people.

We are coming to the end of our conversation and I ask Selma if she has any tree stories she would like to share. She points to the front door and says that the large cherry tree was a gift from Mendel Robinson, a colleague from her garden design days when she first opened the restaurant.

Selma:
"That tree has been a blessing and a curse. We love it. It is magnificent in its youthful, pink spring bloom. And in winter, the branches are gnarled and knotty like old women. But the roots have run through pipes and grown into the foundation causing cracks. The beauty of the tree is worth more than any damage it can create, so I will never cut it down. I believe in the Gaia principle, that the earth is self-healing and we should do as little as possible to harm it. There is joy in the earth."

Noel has been sitting quietly and I ask if she would like to share any stories. She does and begins by emphasizing the importance of the seasons and how we are influenced by external factors when they change.

Noel:
"That is how we cook. We create meals according to what is seasonally grown. Doing this connects us to the struggles and celebrations that are experienced in nature. We've

*Bloodroot Collective Records (MS 1955). Manuscripts and Archives, Yale University Library.

created several cookbooks, but in The *Political Palate*, we included a photo that I took back in 1975. If you have the book, maybe you noticed it. It's a self-portrait that was taken in the fall. I was home in my front yard noticing the shadows a maple tree was making on the ground. You can pass by something so beautiful every day and not notice it. But that day, I wanted a stronger connection to the maple tree, and for nature to become part of my spirit. So I held onto a limb with one arm and extended the other towards the trunk while holding onto my camera. I wasn't sure what it would look like, but when I developed it, it was so powerful for me. The silhouette of the tree and the silhouette of my body united to create one form. I named the photo Hecate, who is the Greek goddess of crossroads, paths, and new beginnings. She is sometimes depicted as an old, angry woman. It's important, I think, for women to consider old age when they are young, to understand that it is a natural and fascinating process. Even though the photo of Hecate is over thirty years old, I still feel a connection and find it timeless."

In her early years, Noel made a living as a fashion model. As she began exploring new interests like photography, her role switched from being the subject to being the artist. Noel takes me to the bookstore section and begins rummaging through files until she finds what she is looking for. She pulls out a photograph of a scanty maple tree near a river in the middle of a mature forest. The sun is shining on the maple, creating an image of a glowing heart.

"This one is named Little Tree," Noel tells me. "It's an image of hope."

She could have described the photo in words, but it was more powerful to show me and let it speak for itself. The way the sunlight illuminated that little tree made it center stage, the mature forest melting into the background. That little tree has a great destiny.

Noel searches for a book that has a quote from Susan Leigh Star, a feminist theorist. She wants to share it with me because Susan's words describe how she felt when she took the Hecate photograph. The book cannot be found, so she offers to send it when it resurfaces.

I thank Selma and Noel and give Bella a few more strokes. Making my way out of the parking lot, I see Noel open the front door, a book in hand, waving for me to stop. "I found the quote," she says, as she passes the book through the window. I read it and understand how Noel was connected to Star's experience of finding a maternal figure in a serene tree.

Months later, I am still thinking of The *Political Palate* and where it could be. I scour my shelves, ask my sister if she has absconded with it, accuse my father of throwing it out, and finally, after all this time, find it shoved in the back of a drawer that I habitually never open. On the back cover is a black and white photo of the original Bloodroot Collaborative: Betsey Beaven, Noel Furie, Pat Shea, and Selma Miriam. They look so young and strong standing together in front of the restaurant's now familiar wall of photographs. I open the book and on the opening page I see four black and white photos of the women's mothers, who are the first, and perhaps most important source of sustenance.

THINKING

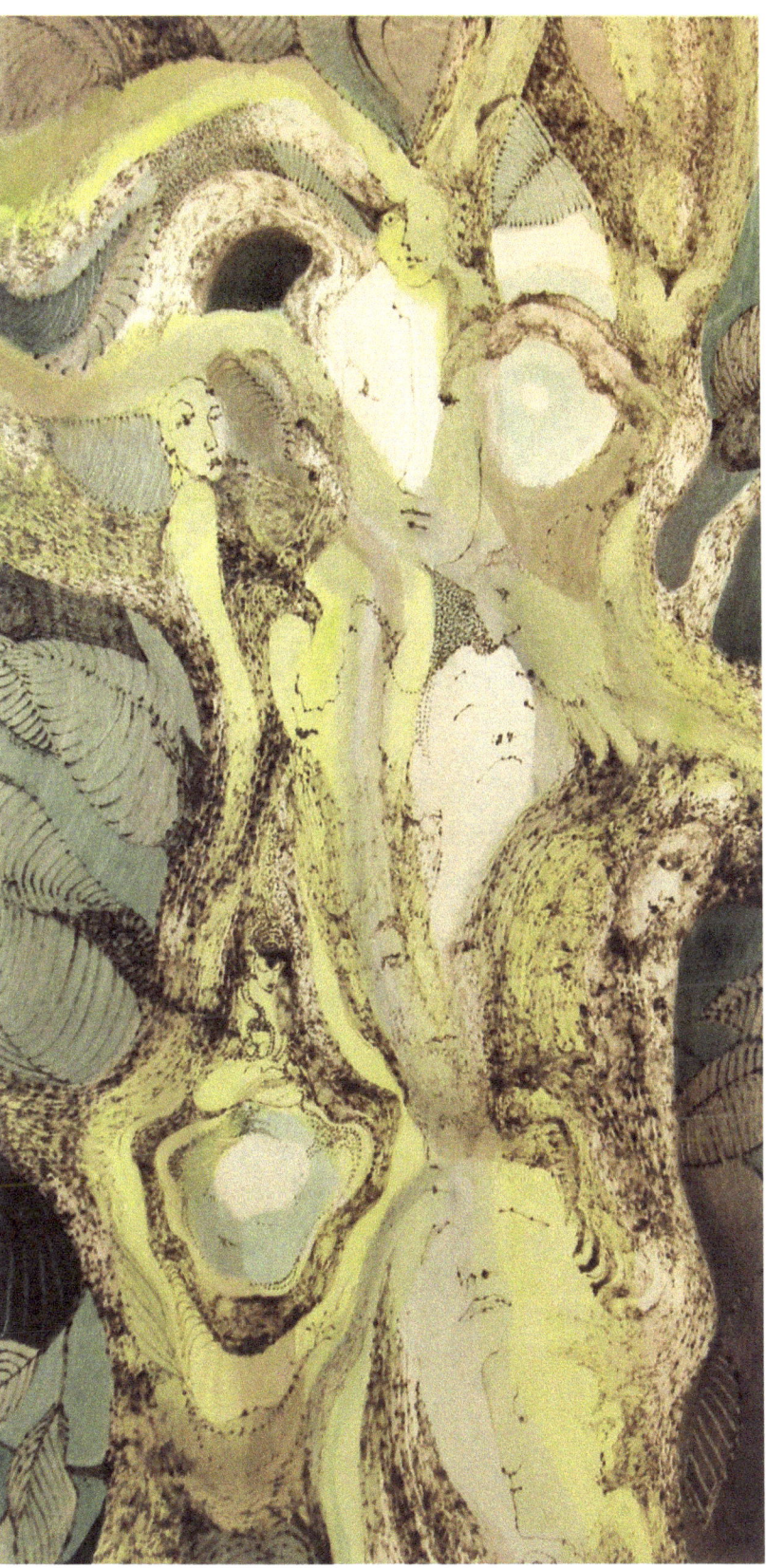

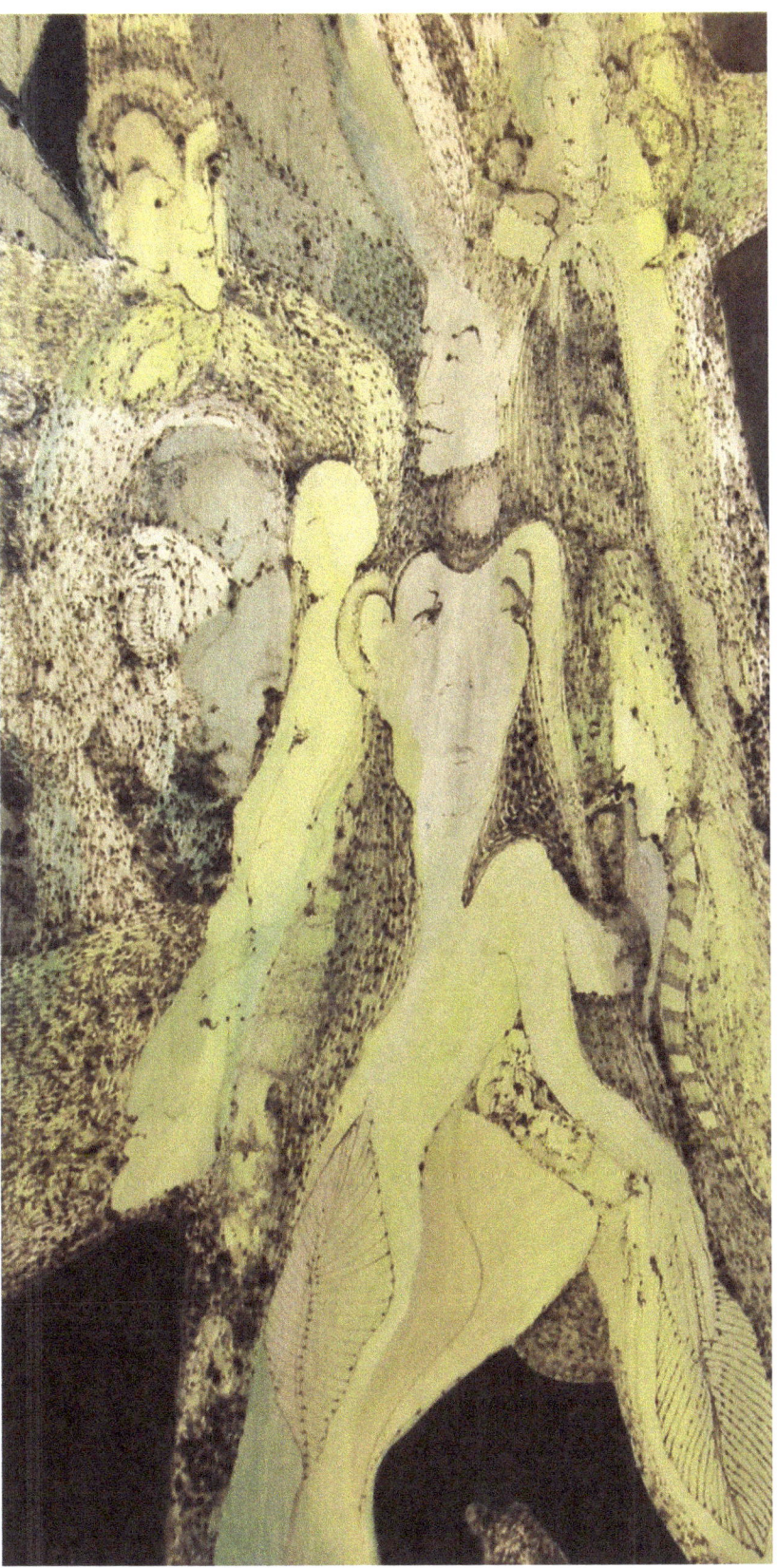

THINKING

Q: Does your center have wings?

A: _____

Ideas grow from seeds of thought,
Safe, at home, then suddenly sparked,
Through trial, through error, and discovery, inquiry, thirst,
Ideas spread like vines into a hungry world.

Thinking craves talking less
And looking more into the eyes of others,
Like a microscope magnifying multi-colored cells,
And seeing bright stars through a telescopic lens.

The process begins with a readiness
To surmise in a spirit of science,
Doubt, believe, and prove:
A rational mind is lost, without the empathy of spirit.

Thinking is fluid, one thought flows to the next
Chartreuse, to emerald, to luscious forest green.
Faces climb in expressive ways:
Smiling eyes, peaked eyebrows, and stolen sideway glances.

Charlatans with snaky thoughts,
Who contemplate Q's and A's
Tempt our will and clip our wings
Propaganda halts invention.

Eric Morgan, Ph.D.

E ric Morgan is a botanist who has spent over twenty years working with plants, studying their structures and identifying their distinctive traits. He has discovered an undiscovered species, that is, a species that has always existed, but lived quietly unknown under a shroud of mystery, deep in the foreign forests of the Amazon. He has given this newly found plant species a name that resonates with its geographical location and the native people who dwell within the forest.

Eric is the scientific progeny in a long line of physicists, analysts, believers of facts, and therefore, atheists. Not that all scientists are atheists, but Eric was raised to believe in not believing. To him, core virtues like honesty, wisdom, justice, and compassion are good values that can be practiced by anyone, anywhere in the world regardless of religious leanings or affiliations.

For almost six years, Eric served as the Bartlett Arboretum's curator of plant collections and director of adult education. His goal, while serving in these posts, was to help the public see as much botanical diversity as possible. Fascinated beyond natural and scientific beauty, Eric has traced ancient cultural connections that have been hidden from the modern world for hundreds of generations, cultural connections he eagerly wants to make accessible to others. By studying plants and the ecosystem we learn about the past and at the same time carve new paths that help create a balance between preservation and innovation.

When Eric and I meet, he tells me he is familiar with the Spirited Trees art project and in the same breath that he does not believe in a God. I assure him that everyone I am speaking with for this book has different belief systems, different backgrounds, and different voices, but what they do have in common is their commitment to building community. As I begin to explain this, a shadow of doubt overcomes me, but I immediately squash it. I know spirit is breath; therefore, every breathing person has a spirit. This is what I believe and so did the many ancients that came before me.

> *Look! Look! Look deep into nature and you will understand everything.*
>
> *~Albert Einstein*

Our identities are often created based on what we believe, so speaking with someone who believes something different can be challenging. A barrier goes up and people quickly become offended or defensive. But surprisingly, this is not the case with Eric. As we connect, our conversation quickly becomes a life lesson in searching, finding, and searching again. I learn that speaking with someone who has different beliefs (or in Eric's case, a lack of beliefs) can lead to an unexpected understanding, one that transcends scientific facts and figures and can open a portal to self-discovery.

Having made eight trips into the Amazon, Eric has lots of stories to share. In 2002, he took his first expedition to Iquitos, Peru, which is the largest city that sits on the Amazon River in the Peruvian rainforest and one of the most botanically diverse places on earth. He gives details, facts and figures all the way down to its latitudinal position, which is four degrees south of the equator.

Eric:
"Iquitos is a modern city and capital of the Loreto region. It has about half a million inhabitants, mostly of a Mestizo background, which is a mix of Spanish European descendants and native Peruvian Indians. It takes eleven hours to reach Iquitos by boat and is the most remote area in the Amazon that borders Peru and Brazil. I travel to Iquitos every year

and more and more I see how different it is from the previous visit. There is less and less rain; therefore, there is less and less rainforest. I see more boats filled with oil and timber. As I move deeper and deeper into the forest, I notice the facility with which cell phones continue to work, ringing even in the heart of the Amazon. . Because I frequently travel back and forth, it is easy for me to recognize trails, so I know my way around the local rivers very well and can see immediately how they have changed. Even though I notice these changes, I am still always struck by the vastness of the rainforest. I initially started to go to South America to study arum plants, which are a part of the Araceae family. There are over four thousand species in this family and some of the more common ones are jack-in-the-pulpit, lords-and-ladies, the peace lily, skunk cabbage, anthurium, philodendron, and the cuckoopint. The corpse flower, which has a horrible fetid scent, is also part of this plant family. Certain arums can actually change their scent to attract different insect groups. I am fascinated by their complex pollination process and how beetles, flies, and other insects are an integral part to the future existence of another species."

Eric paints a vivid backdrop filled with descriptive details. As he speaks, I envision a misty verdant rainforest transforming into a green sea, and vines and trees so entangled that it is difficult to distinguish where one begins and another ends. I hear pulsating sounds that come from fragile, lace-like wings and a constant chorus of sizzling insect songs from cicadas, crickets, and katydids, interrupted by an occasional caw of a horned screamer.

Eric:
"I was interested in understanding how the Iquitos people used the dracontium species so I interviewed two elders from the two local tribes who are curanderos, which means folk healer or shaman. I learned that the most indigenous natives,

the ones that live deepest in the Amazon and farthest from civilization, use the plant in such a way that a spiritual nature has been attached to it. Believing that dracontium protects against snakebites, they whip the plant against their legs and create lacerations that mimic the leaves' veined patterns.

This practice is more like a ceremonial ritual to guard against evil than perhaps really guarding against snakebites. Then we studied an intermediate Mestizo group of people who live on the outskirts of the rainforest. They use dracontium to treat snakebites because they believe it offers a slight benefit to fight inflammation. Then we went into the modern city where the plant is used in a more contemporary medical way by utilizing it to treat AIDS and cancer. Unfortunately, there is no true medicinal value to this plant and I sympathize with all three scenarios. I see how everyone is searching for answers in nature to relieve both spiritual and medical ailments. A few years ago, in 2006, I traveled back to this area of Peru with Jon Sperling, a fellow botanist friend of mine. As we were traveling along the Orosa River, we were forced to stop because a tree had fallen on our path, so we decided to explore the banks as we waited for help. We were gathering plants when we noticed a dracontium species that had similar characteristics to the others but this one was slightly different. The leaf pattern was unusual and the stem had a mix of large and small leaves. We decided to take it back to New York. For eighteen months, we grew and monitored the plant in the Bartlett Arboretum greenhouse and realized it was a new dracontium species. We named it Dracontium iquitense after Iquitos."

There is an element of surprise in science. There is discovery. There is knowledge. There is collaboration. There are solutions. And there is meaning. Creating meaningful experiences, finding the beauty in nature and in humanity, science can lead to spirituality and a greater appreciation beyond any one system. For Eric, it was a fallen tree, a blocked path, and his vibrantly inquisitive nature that led to a wonderful new discovery.

Closer to home, Eric has been investigating the spread of invasive plants in the Bartlett's woodlands and working on a statistical algorithmic model that will help to understand their speed of growth and where they will predominately pervade. He sketches graphs of analysis trends for me and half-joking, half-serious says that maybe an economic solution to the recession can be found in the forests.

> Eric:
> "Invasives can be just as damaging to a native ecosystem as cutting down whole forests. No doubt that these non-native aggressive plant species alter native flora and fauna communities. Even though it is important to witness the biodiversity in nature, it is also important for people to recognize native plants and distinguish the difference between what should be growing in the garden and what should not. It's about being attentive. Invasive plants can strangle the natives and completely change the landscape, making the ecosystem vulnerable to collapse by altering the soil chemistry and actually limiting biodiversity. There is still so much to be discovered. My goal in studying ecology is to understand how species relate to each other, how nature evolves and adapts, and what gets lost in the process."

And here we are. In the snap of a finger, the ecosystem can collapse just like the economy did. There is a relationship between these two ecos, which are each comprised of many infinitesimal parts. Can we understand the workings of a single body part (like the heart or the brain) in isolation from all the others that make up a whole organism? Examining our role in a vast ecosystem and global economy requires humility and an openness to discover balanced, reciprocal relationships with others, our environment, our finances, our culture, and most importantly, ourselves. It requires picking ourselves up from a fall and really examining our actions, behaviors, and thoughts, and asking, "how can I replenish what has been given to me?"

LEARNING

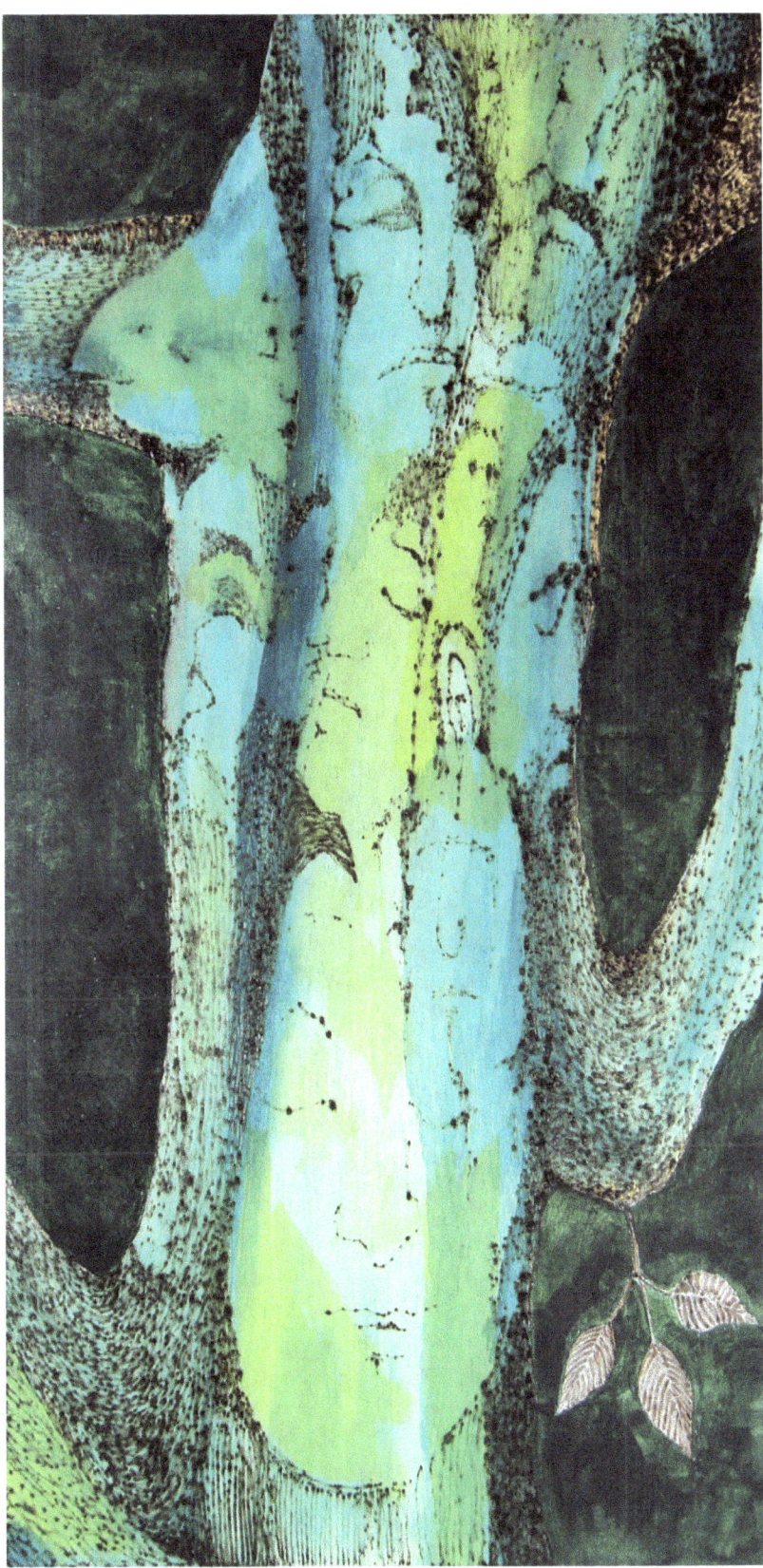

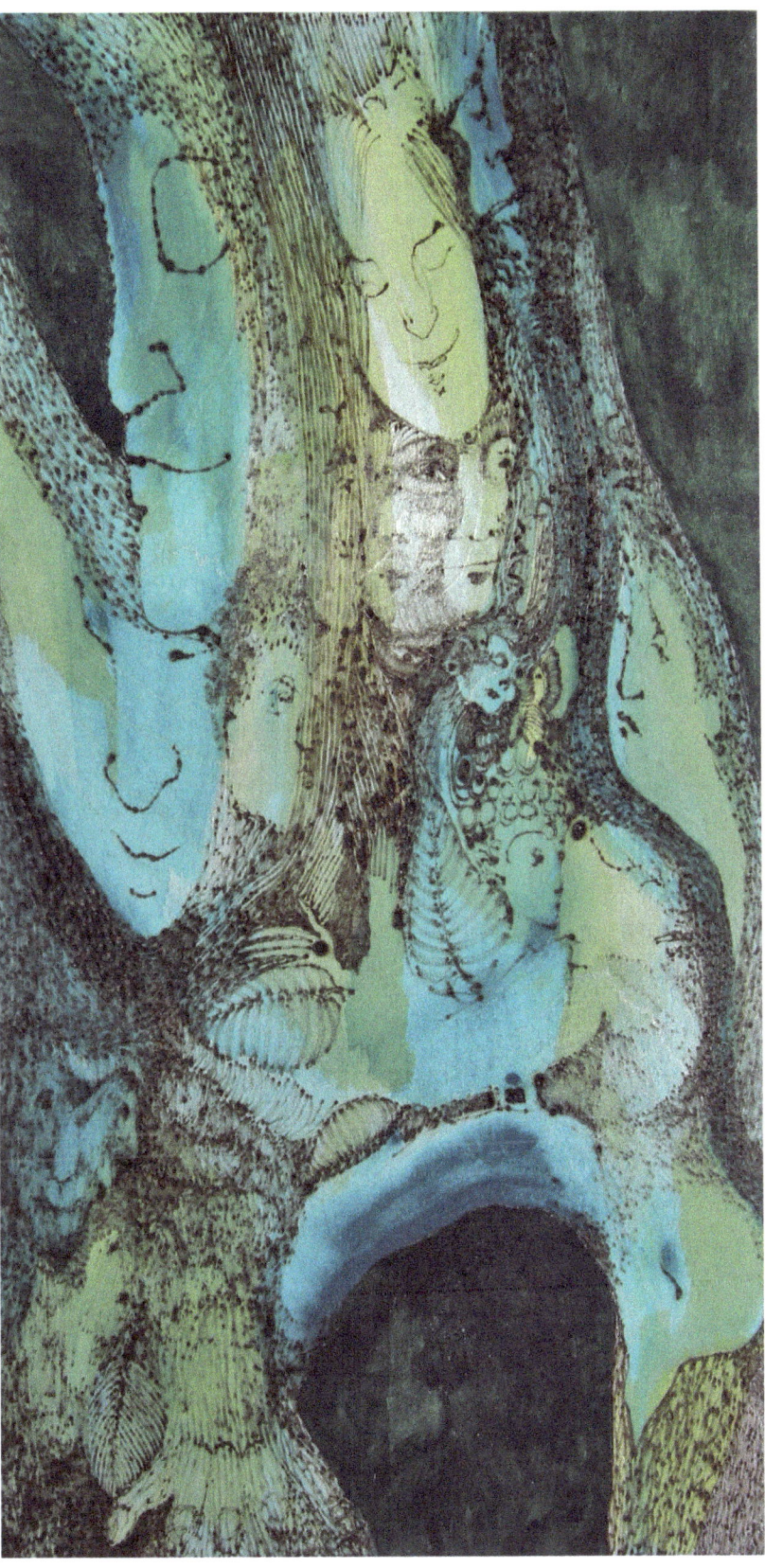

LEARNING

Q: What can we learn from what we already know?
A: _____

Reading books, sharing talk,
Imitating behavior in the dark
We find a steady source of light
And grow higher thoughts to illuminate our souls.

Crawling and clawing like lizards,
Closest to the ground,
We begin to grasp our environment,
Looking up from our hands and knees.

Slowly we evolve
Into sophisticated creatures
Decoding signs, interpreting symbols

Into performance, speech, and memory.
Learning from each other,
From history, from nature
Leaves morph into faces,
Reading, reflecting into clear, glass mirrors.

Learning much from our elders,
Warriors, leaders, who shepherd the many,
Out of the night and towards the moon,
So all can be born in light.

Rev. Msgr. Stephen M. DiGiovanni, H.E.D.

I t is Wednesday, November 3rd, 2010. I am in the heart of downtown Stamford attending the noon mass at the Basilica of St. John the Evangelist, after which, I will be meeting Monsignor DiGiovanni in the sacristy to ask him about his connection to community. I know how busy he is (even though he is too gracious to admit it), so I tell him ours will be a quick meeting, "Fifteen minutes at most," I say.

> We know the truth, not only by reason, but by the heart.
>
> ~Blaise Pascal, Pensées

"For Catholics, the cross is the new tree of life. Jesus is the true vine and his followers are his branches. Jesus gives life by dying on a tree. Yet, we can continue to bear fruit." Monsignor speaks quickly, clearly, slowly, and deeply all at the same time; his voice comes from a spiritual center, his core existence. During our brief interview, he barely speaks a word about himself, only in response to some background questions like where he grew up and when he became a priest. He answers these like simple facts on a timeline, offering a year and then an abbreviated tidbit: born in Boston, raised in Fairfield, Connecticut, and ordained in 1977. Conversely, his charitable actions are like exclamations loudly reverberating throughout the community. Those who admire his work tell others, sharing that he has helped many people by providing food, clothing, housing, work, and guidance, covering every human and spiritual need. There is a cryptic quality to this because his work is his life; it is a holy one.

I have been attending St. John's for several years and

sometimes, during busy workdays, retreat to its old, stone walls for quiet contemplation and to read the story-telling stained glass windows. Outside, the noise of traffic persists, but inside, it is miraculously quiet, and I become deeply absorbed by the silence. Masses are offered here every day, just as they are offered in other churches all over the world. The same readings, the same words, the same themes, all echo through these thick, stone walls built from a local quarry. Day after day, year after year, the same words are spoken and repeated, words falling to the ground like apple seeds from the sky.

> *We must preserve our sacred places in order to know our place in time, our reach to eternity.*
>
> *~N. Scott Momaday, The Man Made of Words*

Monsignor DiGiovanni:
"We welcome everyone here. Every community needs a sacred space for quiet contemplation, for people to be alone with their thoughts and with God. Respecting individuals in the image and likeness of God is how we can bring peace to ourselves and to others. If we love God first, we can relate to other people because we will see God in them. This requires keeping an open mind so that we continue to grow in spirit. It requires practicing forgiveness of past mistakes so that we can grow in compassion. It requires strengthening new generations so they can grow in hope. These are the fruits that we can pluck from the new tree of life."

St. John the Evangelist is considered the "Mother Church" of Stamford. It was established in 1847, a time in history when animosity towards Catholics began to wane and they could freely celebrate the mass, which had been prohibited in the 1700s. A few decades earlier, there was an increased influx of Catholic Irish immigrants, many of whom were criminals and indentured servants. The growing demand for railroad workers coupled with Ireland's devastating potato famine, compelled many to migrate to America with the hope of creating a better life.

As the Irish community grew in Fairfield County, so did the desire to practice their beliefs and by 1875 the present stone church began to rise on Atlantic Street. For over a century, a long line of Irish priests presided over St. John's. So in 1998, when Monsignor Stephen DiGiovanni was appointed pastor, long-time parishioners only heard a foreign last name and balked at his maternally half-Irish heritage. But with time, they warmed up to his presence and hospitably welcomed him into this house of God. It is an Irish tradition to accept all strangers because they believe Christ dwells in everyone.

In 2010, Monsignor was unanimously selected to lead the St. Patrick's Day Parade as the grand marshal for having made St. John's the spiritual center of downtown Stamford. The parade is about honoring tradition and celebrating roots, an event where individuals symbolically walk the same route every year and come together to create one, continuous line of community.

Monsignor holds a deep appreciation for history and art and he injects his homilies with nuggets of wisdom connecting the past to the present. Over the past few years, he led a restoration project: Beautiful murals painted in the 1920s that were later hidden and covered over in creamy white were about to be given a second chance. What seemed to be a piece of history completely erased, actually lay asleep, and was lovingly resurrected during holy week, April 2012.

Gradually, the altar and transepts were uncovered revealing a glowing ceiling of celestial blue overlaid with white lace-like latticework. Vermillion red decorated in gold foliage and symbolic images of Christ as the Lamb of God, the Holy Spirit, and the four holy gospels surround the stained glass windows. Emerald green walls covered in gold fleur-de-lis mimic an endless meadow. Once the altar was complete, the murals spread to the side walls, thirteen arches, and supporting columns, creating a spiritual landscape inside the basilica. For years, the walls looked like blank pages, but now, they are filled with biblical stories and symbols, a spectacular architectural and spiritual wonder. Opening the doors to St. John the Evangelist is like opening a treasure chest, gleaming with jewel-toned colors covered in an ever-reaching gold vine.

History is a symphony of echoes heard and unheard. It is a poem with events as verses.

~Charles Angoff

Monsignor DiGiovanni:
"This church was built by our ancestral parishioners, and now, the restoration of its murals was made possible through the generosity of its present ones. It is a gift for everyone, the Stamford community, and the global Catholic community. We have uncovered the beauty of a past generation of Catholics that once worshiped here. Beauty, truth, and charity lead to the essence of God."

Rabbi Joseph Ehrenkranz

September's crisp sunshine warmed my kitchen as I sat sipping pomegranate green tea, flipping through a local newspaper. A headline fortuitously caught my eye: "SHU CCJU To Honor Rabbi Ehrenkranz with Nostra Aetate Award." Having no idea what it meant, I read the article and decided I had to absolutely meet with this extraordinary man.

> A society grows great when old men plant trees whose shade they know they shall never sit in.
>
> ~Greek Proverb

Issued by Fairfield's Sacred Heart University Center for Christian-Jewish Understanding, The Nostra Aetate Award (which means "of our times") recognizes world leaders who embody spirit, embolden dialogue, and cultivate practices of sincere inter-religious encounters that foster religious harmony and world peace. The award was named after the Second Vatican Council's concluding document (1965), in which Pope Paul VI proclaimed the Church no longer held Jews responsible for the death of Jesus. It also set the Catholic Church on a vigorous path toward dialogue and understanding with other faiths.

Through a series of emails and phone calls, I was granted fifteen minutes to meet with Rabbi Ehrenkranz on October 14th at the Greenwich Hyatt, the very same evening that he would be receiving the Nostra Aetate honor. And now, here we are on this misty crepuscule, sitting on chairs in front of the reception room doors, in a public passage that feels so private. A glowing presence emanates from the rabbi's smiling eyes. They are kind and welcoming and I am immediately put at ease. As I follow the gently creased lines of his folded hands, I begin to retrace all the kind individuals who guided me to him, and I feel a deep sense of gratitude. I extend my hand to offer my congratulations and thank him for this time.

I ask him about receiving the Nostra Aetate Award and he tells me that his peers and members of the community bestowed it as recognition for his global scale efforts to cultivate peace. After many years of representing the Synagogue Council of America before the United Nations, and meeting with popes, diplomats, and international leaders, he retired and moved to Tel Aviv, Israel, but has now returned to Stamford—a place where he feels his roots run deep—to receive this honorable award.

I explain the Spirited Trees project to him and he responds by sharing the biblical verse "man is tree" and says there are many of these types of references. In Micah 4:4, for example, reference to both the tree and vine are united, "Everyone will live in peace and prosperity, enjoying their own grapevines and fig trees, for there will be nothing to fear."* Peace grows when one can live without fear. A simple concept, but one the world has yet to fully embrace.

He tells me about his father, who was also an orthodox rabbi and helped people to live better lives and to build better communities, and from whom he believes he received the penchant for organizing and aiding others. After completing his rabbinical studies in 1949, the rabbi was assigned to lead the Agudath Sholom Synagogue in Stamford.

Rabbi Ehrenkranz:
"Do you know which synagogue it is? It's on Strawberry Hill in Stamford, the one across from St. Bridget's Church. I started my peace work there by reaching out to our neighbors. Father Nagle was the pastor of St. Bridget's at the time, and we organized inter-religious events between the Catholic and Jewish congregations. We offered lectures, fundraisers, and

dinner dances. The events started out small, but attendance just kept growing and everyone had so much fun and experienced so much healing. After centuries and centuries of tense relations, we began reconciling with each other. It was only a local reconciliation, but it represented so much more. Those events made me realize there was a need for diverse religious communities to communicate. We couldn't simply live across the street from one another and pretend like the other did not exist. People want peace and becoming friends is a start. In 1990, I was asked to serve as a delegate to the Vatican. There were twenty Jewish representatives and twenty Catholic representatives studying the value of inter-religious dialogue. I realized we needed to learn a new language—a spiritual one. At the end of conference, Pope John Paul II asked to meet individually with each of us. It was my first time there, so I decided to take the last place in line. When it was my turn, he graciously welcomed me and we connected like old friends. I felt great respect for him. I invited him to come to Israel; he accepted and traveled several times to join me there. I remember having a few moments with him alone before he went out to conduct mass at the cathedral in Nazareth. We could hear the crowd outside chanting, 'JP2, we love you!' beckoning him to come out so they could have a glimpse of him. We were standing together in a doorway looking out at the expansive landscape below and I said to him, 'I'm going to plant a forest of a million trees here in your honor.' Tu Bishvat, or New Year for Trees, is a Jewish holiday that occurs in late January or early February, depending on when three stars are visible in the sky, and is a time to celebrate the ground coming alive to nurture trees, especially fruit trees, and the way trees grow from the earth's elements. Children often go door to door asking for money so

* The Book of Micah, 4:4

that they can plant new trees. In Jewish tradition, we allow trees to grow three years without plucking the fruit. The fourth year, we offer the fruit as a gift to God, and then in the fifth, we harvest. It is a smart way to calculate the age of trees and also to give thanks for the gift of fruit. When I went to Rome in 1990, I was starting to think about retirement, but

> A person is a person through other persons. You can't be human in isolation. You are human only in relationships.
>
> ~Archbishop Desmond Tutu

that meeting with Pope John Paul II ignited a peace fire within me. My search to find a local place where I could do peace work led me to Anthony Cernera, Sacred Heart University's president at the time. When I explained my vision to him, I could see the enthusiasm in his eyes. In 1992 we founded the CCJU so we could develop inter-religious dialogue and work towards peace. Undoubtedly, we need to expand the dialogue further and invite Muslims into the circle. I believe global peace will come. It may take hundreds of years, but it will come. You should contact Anthony Cernera, he can tell you more about the CCJU."

Dr. Anthony J. Cernera

D r. Cernera, who served as president of Sacred Heart University for twenty-two years, has had the honor of meeting with Pope Benedict XVI more than six times, and convened with Pope John Paul II more than ten times in private five-person assemblies to discuss Judeo-Christian issues. If that were not enough, he experienced a once in a lifetime opportunity to bask in the compassionate presence of Mother Theresa. And of course, co-founded the Center for Christian-Jewish Understanding with Rabbi Ehrenkranz. Not knowing much about me, the project, Kathy's art, or why I would like to speak with him, Dr. Cernera still carved out a chunk of time to get together with me on what is perhaps the busiest, most traffic-filled day of the year—the Wednesday afternoon before Thanksgiving Day.

I arrive a few minutes late and find Dr. Cernera sitting and waiting, quietly reading. I am embarrassed that he has had to wait for me, but his calm, humble, and soft-spoken manner immediately erases my shame.

He begins by talking about the creation of the CCJU, and how a group of local people, who wanted to weave the concept of inter-religious understanding into the university's mission, was instrumental in its creation. Dr. Cernera grew up in the Bronx in a largely Jewish Italian dichotomy. By the age of thirteen, he had been to fourteen bar mitzvahs, a traditional celebration that marks the transition from boy to man and a time when one becomes morally responsible for his actions.

Dr. Cernera's mention of being responsible makes me consider the actual word, how deceptive it can be. As one matures, there is a natural tendency to acquire more responsibility. But who wants more responsibility now? Who wants more burdens? Who wants to assume more duties and relinquish their own precious time of which we seem to have so much less of these days? It is never ending.

> God speaks in the silence of the heart. Listening is the beginning of prayer.
>
> ~Blessed Mother Theresa of Calcutta

Many young people rebel from responsibility; they want freedom - freedom from duties and obligations and to do as they please. But is this really what freedom means? Or could it be that we can find genuine freedom through embracing pious responsibility?

This was the case for Dr. Cernera. This idea of being morally responsible permeated his thinking in his early life. Attending Catholic schools and learning theology was not enough, so he began practicing through fellowship, becoming actively involved in a community of faith through volunteer work. But it was Viktor E. Frankl's *Man's Search for Meaning** that really ignited him. Frankl chronicles an autobiographical account of his days spent in the brutality of a World War II concentration camp, and the thoughts that occupied his mind during that time, like how some were able to survive the horrific nightmare while others perished.

Frankl questioned and questioned and came to the conclusion that his life had purpose beyond the impenetrable walls, beyond the senseless suffering, beyond the heart-wrenching anguish. He found meaning, even in all of that anguish, and therefore, he must will himself to survive.

Dr. Cernera:
"Studying war, the Holocaust, and how the lives of real people were affected by others' decisions made me realize that my own thoughts, words, and actions have a great impact on

society and the world beyond myself. I was irrevocably moved. The stories, the real stories, and there are so many, made me promise that I would be responsible for life, my own, and my fellow man's. I remember reading about an Austrian catholic peasant named Franz Jägerstätter who refused to round up Jews and fight in the war. He wanted to discuss the morality of the war with his bishop, but the bishop did not want to confront these issues. When he was called to serve in the war, Franz still refused, and was later imprisoned and beheaded. Learning about Franz made me promise to do something to improve inter-religious relations. When I was a junior at Fordham University, I started a soup kitchen near campus called Bread for the World. It was run by students and we not only prepared meals for the homeless and the hungry, but we advocated for them by writing letters to Congress, requesting government assistance in continuing programs to aid those in need, campaigning for international development to reduce poverty. We had the power to influence public policy for a group of citizens who are voiceless and therefore, never heard. Hunger is an injustice issue that is often dealt with through acts of charity. A small act of kindness and generosity can make a world of difference in someone's life. Every day we have opportunities to perform such small acts. I had been fortunate to meet with Mother Theresa on several occasions and I immediately knew that I was in the presence of a holy woman. She glowed a radiance of kindness in the most abject poverty. She made me feel bigger than myself. My group meetings with Pope John Paul II to discuss improving inter-religious dialogue had a similar effect and made me feel as though I was interacting with a presence that was bigger than myself. When Pope John Paul II died, I attended his funeral and sat with the Jewish delegation just a few steps away

*Viktor E. Frankl, Man's Search for Meaning (Boston, Beacon Press, 2006).

from his casket. Surrounded by the pageantry of the ceremony and burial, I felt like I was participating in life completely. I did not see death; I felt life."

> Each man is questioned by life; and he can only answer to life by answering for his own life; to life he can only respond by being responsible.
>
> ~Dr. Viktor Frankl

As we prepare to leave, Dr. Cernera recommends that I read the First Letter of Paul to the Philippians. Months later, I open to these words: "I thank my God in all my remembrance of you, always offering prayer with joy in my every prayer for you all..." It is a prayer of remembrance and thanksgiving. "...if there is any fellowship of the Spirit, if any affection and compassion, make my joy complete by being of the same mind, maintaining the same love, united in spirit, intent on one purpose. Do nothing from selfishness or empty conceit, but with humility of mind regard one another as more important than yourselves; do not merely look out for your own personal interests, but also for the interests of others." * It is a prayer of pious responsibility and achievable unity; this is the thanksgiving harvest.

*The Epistle of St. Paul to the Philippians, 1:1; 2:1-4.

HOLDING

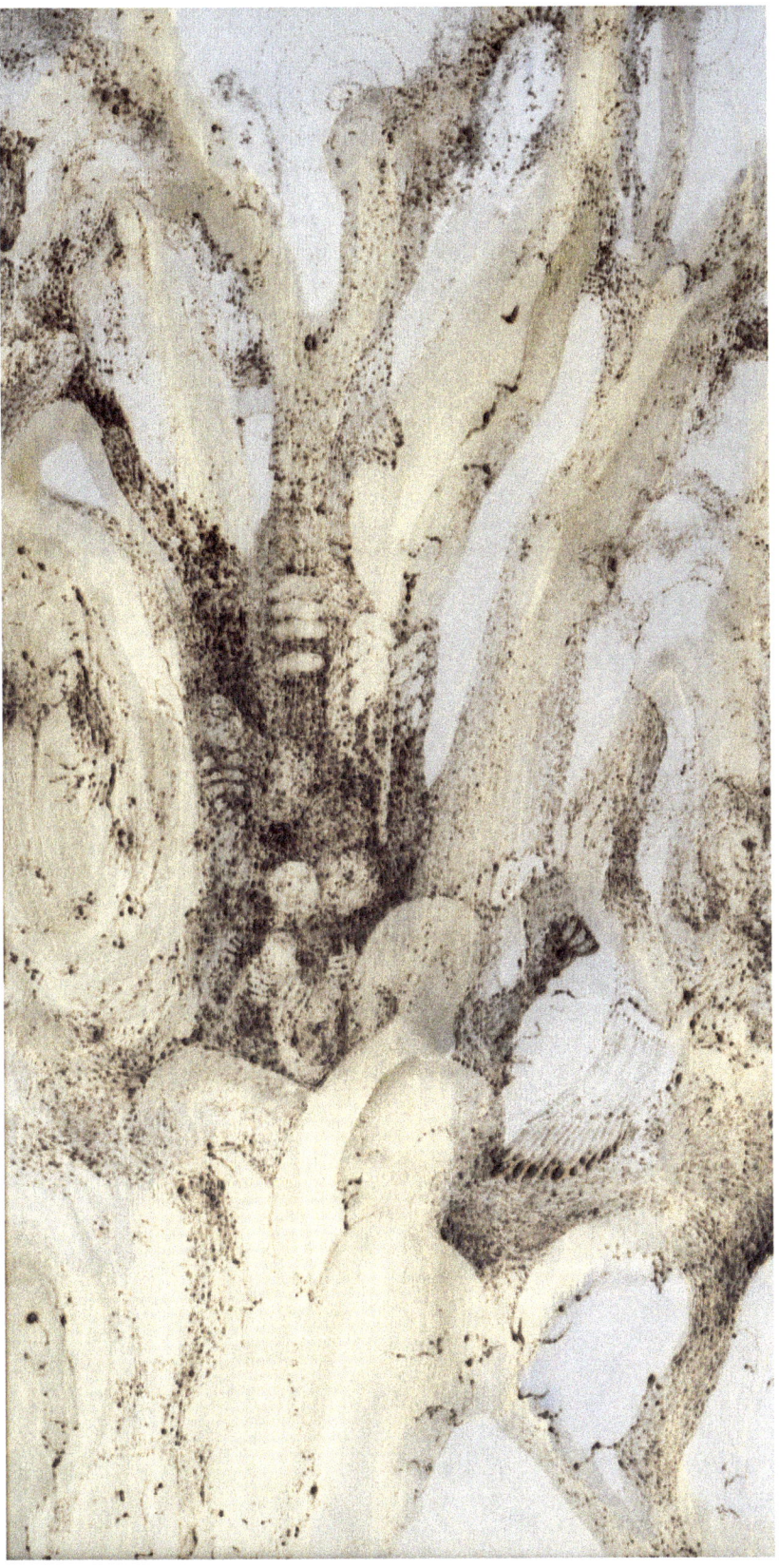

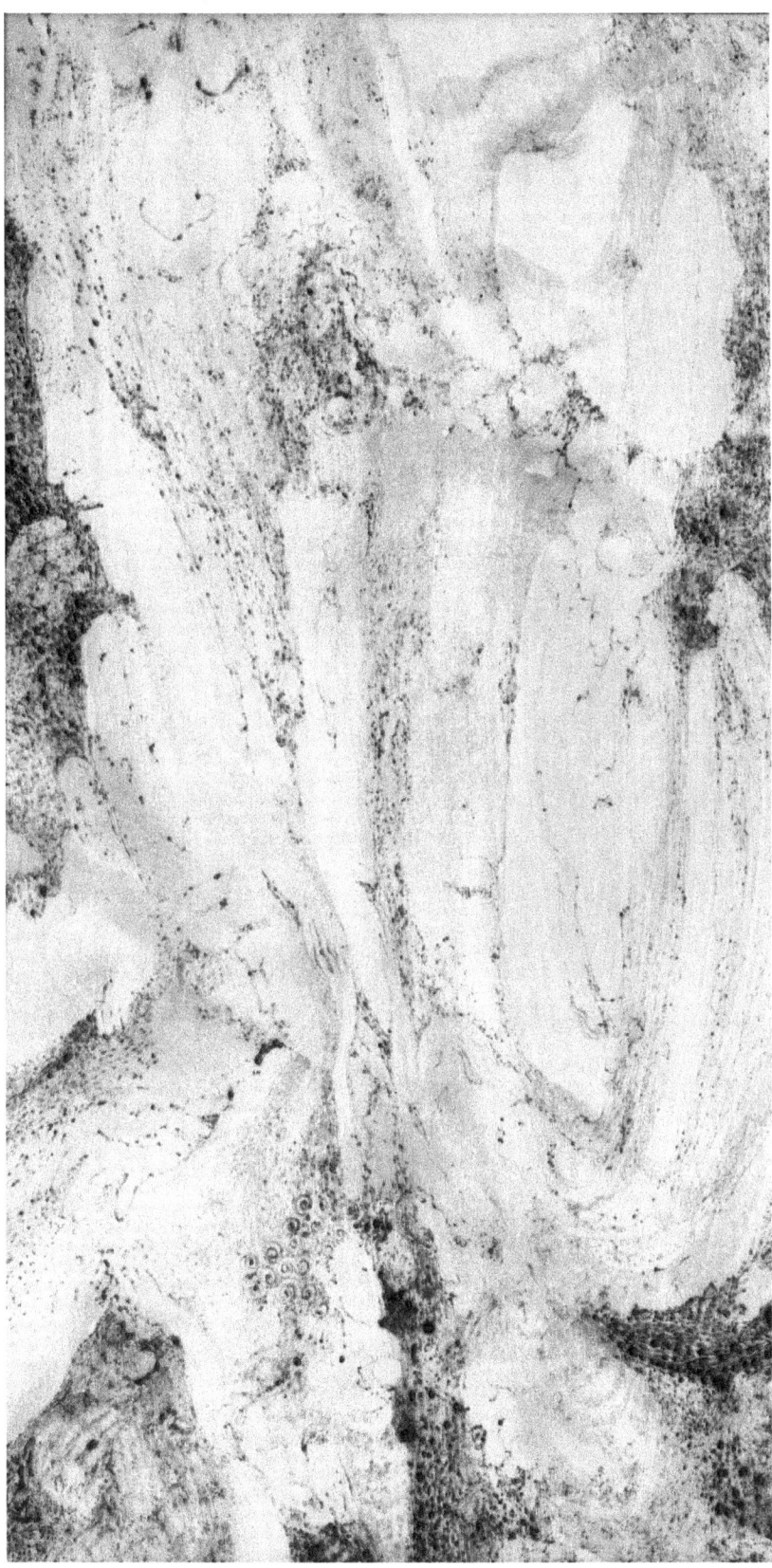

HOLDING

Q: What do you hold that is true?
A: _____

We hold memories, ideals, people, and breath,
Compassion, anger, gazes, and hands,
Photographs, letters, videos, and hope,
Holding is not static, but a living breathing feeling.

Fiercely and gently, folding, melting, flowing,
There is power in holding.
Liquid and airy, we carry,
Our hearts outside our bodies.

Chronicling the journey, cradling the past,
For all the souls with whom we've walked,
And all the ones we shall never meet
Feelings are beliefs transformed into truth.

We are water, and water we hold,
Crossing the arid desert,
With cupped hands and hopeful hearts
Sipping from streams and quenching our thirst.

Holding--celestial blue and copious brown,
A commingling of earth, water, and air.
Rooted in images of prophets praying,
With folded, raised hands, and divine voices praising.

Buddha holding a pearl of wisdom,
Reflecting upon a limitless sky.
Krishna playing his divine flute,
Listen! Sweet music amongst the trees.

Faces holding on to a moment,
Kissing, embracing, then setting it free
Like birds' wings spreading in flight,
Higher, higher, holding our hearts, high.

Abdel Metwally

L ife is complicated," Abdel Metwally tells me. As we sit at Lucky's Diner in downtown Stamford, on this foggy fall day, he quickly shifts the topic, talking about Egypt, his homeland, and begins a political soliloquy that lasts well over an hour. Years and years of history flowing out of him like spilt milk.

I met Abdel at a local networking event in early summer, 2010. He boldly stood out at this intimate gathering; I imagine he would have the same effect standing in a large mass. His voice was foreign, but not only because of his Egyptian accent. It has a slight high pitch, like a male blackbird that cries out to fellow birds over noisy morning traffic then changes its song just so it can be heard. Abdel is like that, changing his song and talking over you so he can hear his own ideas, ensuring you understand him. More than anything, Abdel wants to be understood.

Abdel introduced himself as a writer and shared that his book, *Be Honest to Succeed*,* had just been published. Like a new mother brings her firstborn baby to show family and friends what she has produced, he brought a copy of his first published book.

So proud and rightfully so. Strangers may mistake him as arrogant because he loves to talk--talk politics, talk history, talk business. And he always wants to be right. Unperturbed, I introduced myself anyway, mentioning that I was also writing a book, even though I was not sure if he had understood me at all. He crammed his book into my arms and said, "Read this and let me know what you think. I'm curious to know what you think. Write a review. Call me when you're done."

*Adel Metwally, Be Honest to Succeed (iUniverse Inc., 2008).

I accepted the book and promised I would read it. Be Honest to Succeed was a quick read and a quick review, which I posted to my blog. A week later, I left him a message then sent him an email. Days passed and still no reply. Maybe he was ill. Maybe he was traveling. Maybe he just did not like what I wrote. A few days later, a voice message, a flow of gratitude, and a stream of apologies for not getting back to me sooner; it had been Ramadan. When we finally connected, I told Abdel I wanted to know more about Islam and asked if I could interview him. "Of course, of course, of course," he said, "meet me at Lucky's."

So we meet at Lucky's. He orders a hamburger and I sip on a chocolate milkshake, coincidentally, completely American. I do not need to ask questions; Abdel is happy just to have someone listen. I pick up on tone, key words, and the extreme emphasis on specific phrases. Almost two hours into our conversation, I tell him that I need to stop and feed the meter.

"Alright," he says, "I'll take a break too."

As we walk towards the back door, he pulls out a cigarette from one pocket and from the other, in a fatherly way, offers me change for the parking meter. I graciously decline and let him know I will be right back.

Meter fed, cigarette extinguished, I begin to ask Abdel a few questions about Islam. "Read my second book, *Amenah*,* " he replies. "You'll find everything you need to know there." And when I try and press him again, he says, "I'm working on a third book and you will be able to find more answers there."

Little by little, he lets go of history, politics, and dates, and begins to share more personal points like in his home, the Torah, the Bible, and the Qur'an all sit on the same shelf, at the same level. One is not on top of the other indicating a personal preferred order; rather, all three exist on the same plane.

He invites me to visit his home to see for myself. His offer confuses me. I wanted to know about the symbolism and significance of trees in Muslim culture. But I could not get Abdel to focus and answer my questions.

> *All the art of living lies in a fine mingling of letting go and holding on.*
>
> *~Henry Ellis*

Determined to get some answers, I take him up on his offer. A few weeks later I called Abdel and he said, "I'm so happy to hear from you."

A week later, Abdel and I meet again. This time, I visit the office in his apartment and when I walk in I am amazed at the walls. One is completely covered in wallpaper that depicts an Asian landscape of craggy cliffs, rushing rivers, splashing waterfalls, snow-capped mountains, and knotty bonsai trees. Directly opposite this elaborate composition is another scene: A wall covered in a forest of oaks and maples with endless ribbons of colorful tulips and daffodils threading through the trees. Two different landscapes with Abdel in the middle, his desk positioned at the center of these diverse worlds. Above his head is a shelf with the three equally positioned holy books. He points to them and says, "See, here they are."

Born before the 1967 Six-Day War, Abdel had enjoyed a peaceful childhood in Egypt. No doubt it was difficult, working on his father's farm just outside of Alexandria, but still, it was peaceful. Abdel tells of having Coptic friends, the normalcy that existed between Muslims and Christians, how mosques and churches were friendly neighbors. He remembers American aid packages (boxes similar to those distributed in Europe after World War II) that contained food and medical supplies. On the outside of each package was an image of two hands shaking in friendship and the slogan "Make friends not enemies." What was written outside was more powerful than what was packaged inside. These relief boxes were considered gifts from the

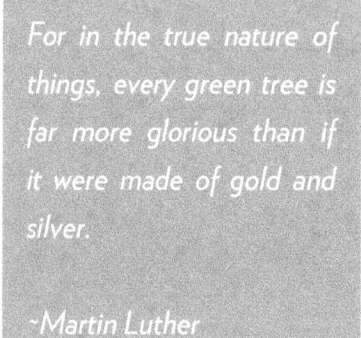

For in the true nature of things, every green tree is far more glorious than if it were made of gold and silver.

~Martin Luther

United States, a gesture of the rich helping the poor on a global level. There was tremendous respect and gratitude towards the United States amongst the Egyptian people. But then the packages stopped coming. Hands dropped, bombs dropped, and war ensued between the Arab nations and Israel. Because the United States supported Israel, everything in Abdel's life changed.

Abdel:
"I didn't understand what was happening. Why was there war? I was young and didn't understand the politics. We lost the war. I felt betrayed and promised myself that I would find the answer. I went to school and there was more war. Tension between Egypt and the United States grew, but I wanted to come here. I wanted to understand what it was like to be American."

Abdel's first book, *Be Honest to Succeed,* is an autobiographical account of how he managed to survive and prosper in the United States. The sacrifices he made and what he learned along the way. A true story that transcends any ethnic affiliation, religious bent, or political preference, the book answers questions like: What is honesty? What is truth? What makes people veer away from it? Honesty, something that seems so simple can actually be quite complex.

Abdel's story begins in 1969, as a part of his life ended and a new one began when he emigrated from Egypt, his fatherland, to the United States, his adopted one. Well-educated in business

* Abdel Metwally, Amenah (Xlibris Corporation, 2010).

from Alexandria University, Abdel was eager to find respectable employment in New York City. His early work experiences proved to be a test of character, often working two jobs at the same time not only to make ends meet, but more importantly, to get ahead.

> Abdel:
> "Going faster and higher seemed easy. Ethically lax colleagues tempted me with plenty of opportunities to make fast money. But I didn't do this. I did not go down that road. I made the right decisions even when it was easier to make the wrong ones. That's how I earned my reputation for honesty. Managers in the hospitality, accounting, and real estate industries would call me for advice. It was very easy for me to give them my honest opinion on how to make their businesses more efficient and profitable. How did I do this? By communicating with employees, by taking a cooperative approach in understanding why their current systems were failing, and figuring out how the organization could achieve higher standards. My aim was to create focus in situations where the company's vision had been lost."

Ahead of his time, Abdel realized a company's "balanced success" was based on the quality of upper management's relationship to its employees and also by the manner in which it conducted business outside the office. Abdel discussed waste in terms of resources, the most precious of these being people and time. He also introduced another concept of waste – environmental. In 1973, studying at Long Island University, Abdel demonstrated that those without a conscience tend to be heavy polluters and show little remorse for the damage they create in his thesis, "The Relationships Between Corporate Management and Environmental Problems." His conclusion was that management's attitude of "sale, sale, sale" can be detrimental to its success if it does not consider the effect its actions have on the environment and community. Abdel can be considered a founder of corporate social responsibility by his monitoring of ethical business practices to ensure a triple bottom line of people, planet, and profits.

Abdel's lessons in honesty and human nature and how they relate to the environment can come across as overly simplified, but there are many truths that fold into each other. Abdel's own journey to success was a slow one. He is an ordinary man working hard, living honestly in the new American reality.

Abdel reminds me of my father: a strong work ethic, a facility with recalling past details like they were yesterday's news, and an intuitive ability to foresee consequences of global events. Not because either of them are of a prophet-like nature, but because they have a keen understanding of human nature. I hear the same struggle and satisfaction in both of their voices.

Amenah, Abdel's second book, is a work of fiction about a woman who suffers a loss of identity. She loses herself in a world that seems to allow for greater freedom than the one in which she is accustomed, only to discover the destruction of social values and morality in her new domain. In the end, Amenah finds herself and her spirit by finding God and all of his beautiful names: The Holy One, The Eternal, The Cherisher, The Sustainer, The Creator.

Abdel:
"There are rules to every religion and I don't promote one set of beliefs over another. It does not matter whether you call yourself Jewish, Christian, or Muslim. It does matter that you follow the rules of the faith you have chosen and that you always believe in the Creator. We come from the same line of Abraham. We can trace this line through history as it passes through different people who believe different things. But we are all still connected."

Standing up and walking over to the western wall landscape,

Abdel points to the trees.

Abdel:
"How can anyone say that God did not create the birds, the trees, and the flowers? Look at how this tree lives! When God sends the rain to the earth, the tree knows to take in the water and grow tall towards the sun. When I visit the park, you know, Binney Park in Old Greenwich? I go there and notice the geese eating and as the sun begins to set, one gander starts swimming away from the others towards the sun. He becomes a leader and the other geese follow. Then they fly off together into the woods, safe from the night. Every time I go to the park, I study how they do this. I really enjoy watching nature because even in my old age, I feel like I am seeing something new. Have you ever seen the birds of paradise mating dance? Wow, what amazing colors! Blue, red, yellow, orange, black--all these bright colors! The male bird dances for the female bird! How does he know how to do this dance? Who taught him? God did. God created nature."

> Observe the wonders as they occur around you. Don't claim them. Feel the artistry moving through and be silent.
>
> ~Rumi

Abdel stomps his feet like a flamenco dancer, extends his arms and flutters in a circle to show me the birds of paradise dance. We laugh and laugh. "Eat more cookies," he says, pushing a plate of chocolate covered coconut macaroons my way.

Abdel's third book, Kefayah, Sickness of Power,* takes its name from the Egyptian democratic movement. Kefayah means "enough" in Arabic, a sentiment echoed in the 2011 Egyptian uprisings to overthrow President Mubarak's regime. Abdel feels that Americans are also growing tired of legislative lies and encourages everyone to

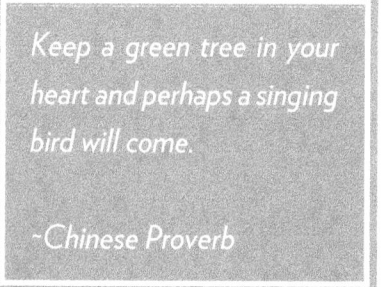

act in a way that restores social and economic morals. In other words, be honest. In all three of his books, Abdel reflects on the need to return to the truth.

Abdel:
"Humans are the only creatures that challenge God. From the beginning of mankind, there were stories of civilizations turning their back on God. These people were destroyed by floods, fires, earthquakes, all types of disasters.

But there were ruins left behind, like the pyramids in Egypt and the columns in Rome. Those ruins were left behind to remind us that those who went before us, who thought they were so great, do not exist anymore.

It is a humbling lesson to visit ruins because we realize that one day we will also die. But sometimes, we foolishly hold on to the belief that maybe we will not die. That we are somehow greater than God. We are not greater than God. We are exactly the same as the ones that came before us."

Abdel gives me answers by reciting parables from the bible and simple stories from his own life. I can tell he is someone who is used to holding on to feelings, beliefs, and ideas, but he finally lets go so that I may find my own answers. The last story he shares is over a decade old, one where he stepped off a Metro North train at Stamford and saw a crowd on the platform surrounding a politician he did not care to follow. The politician was smiling, sharing small talk, and shaking hands with everyone.

Abdel:
"I remember he extended his hand to me and I refused to take it. I walked away. But still now, many years later, I

think about that day. I realize I should have not walked away. I should have stopped and asked him questions. If that ever happens to me again, I will stop and shake the person's hand. I will stop and ask questions."

*Abdel Metwally, Kefayah, Sickness of Power (Xlibris Corporation, 2011)

OFFERING

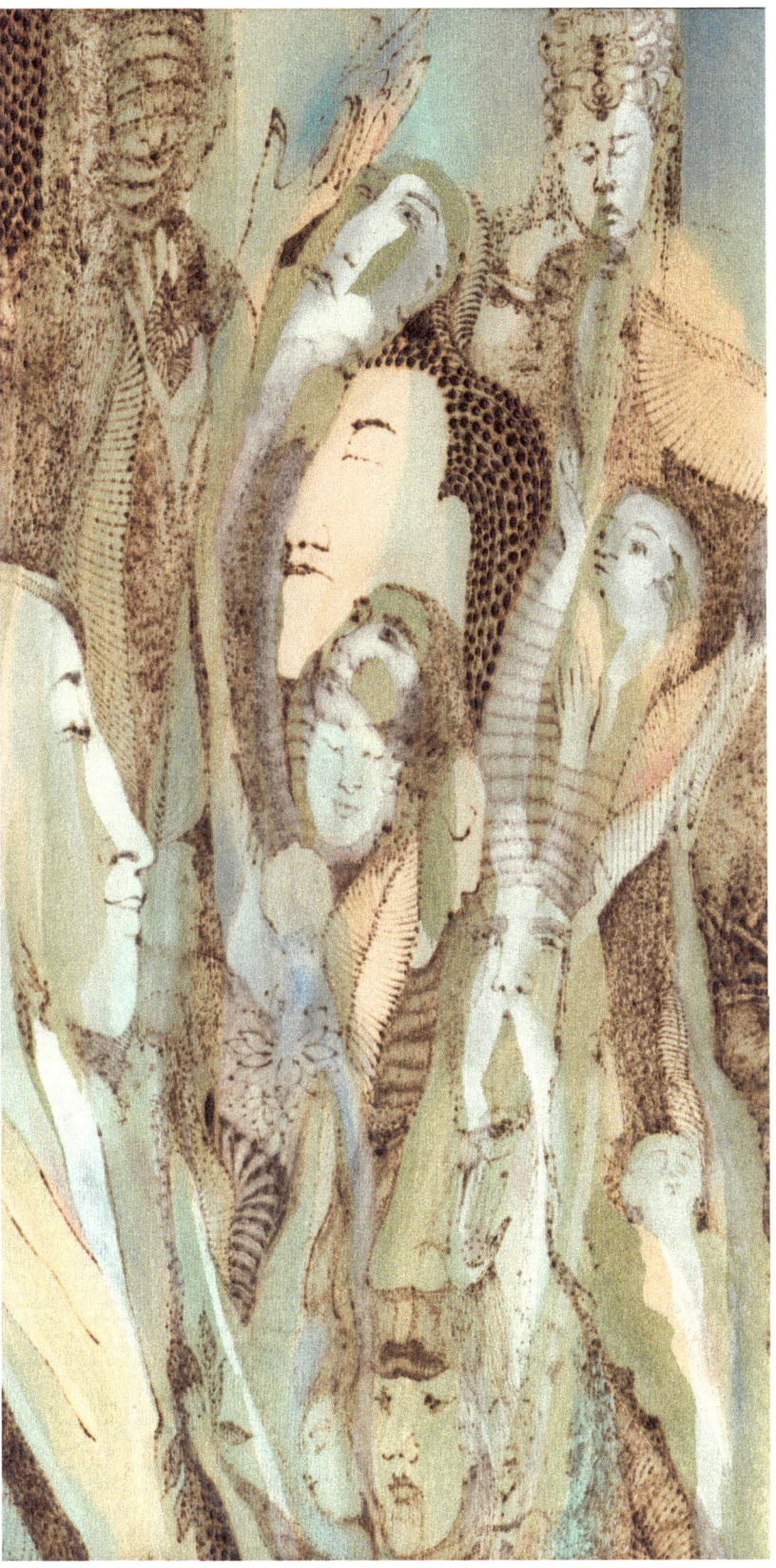

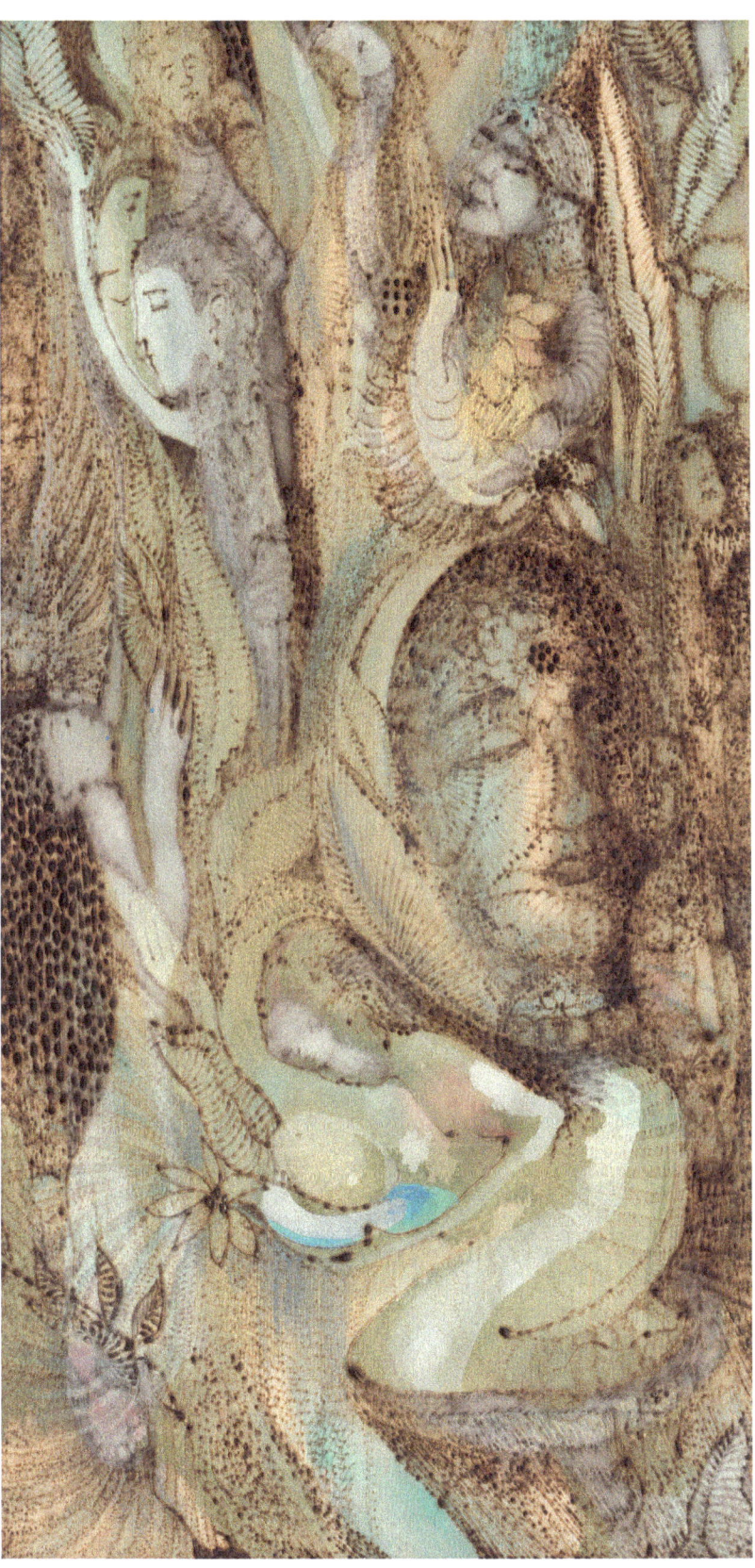

OFFERING

Q: Do you give in grace?
A: _____

Today offers an opening,
To grow and learn, to love and become
Offering is freely giving, and concurrently,
Receiving grace for self, selflessly.

Offerings were once sacrificial rites
Demonstrating devotion, gratitude, repentance
Plumes of smoke rose to heaven from earth,
See? Our ancestors sacrificed in plenty, but today, not as much.

Is there a need to keep on offering?
A need for something greater?
Whose essence craves the heart and mind,
Conjoin through thoughts, acts, and prayers.

Offering cannot be neglected,
For temporal notions like success,
Mistakenly viewed as deserving of praise
Successes fail; false beliefs have value no longer.
 And then? There is pain and loss and suffering--oh, how we hurt!

We can learn from this gift of failure,
By offering a helping hand,
Securing something better, greater, for a not too distant future.

Offering is sunrise,
Green with blue, and streaks of pink and golden light.
A young girl bowing over a sacred seed,
Unfurling like a leaf--half human, half sylvan.

Over forty faces born from this seed,
With arms that form stalwart branches--they are the Offering Tree.
A woman wearing a tilaka, becomes a lotus flower,
Blooming in morning, closing at night, the goddess of rebirth.

There are many faces in Offering,
Whose eyes are shut, but fully awake,
Who joyfully rise and greet the day,
With helping hands and signs of peace: a song, a flower, a prayer.

Offering is an on-going path,
One walked every day, every hour, every moment
And at the end you ask again,
"What can I offer you tomorrow?"

Sandra E. Angulo

A friend invited me to attend a meditation group led by Sandra Angulo, founder of Sacred Doors, a healing and education center in Norwalk, Connecticut that teaches body, mind, spirit connectedness and wholeness. The center's mission is to empower individuals "to regenerate by going back to the roots of our being, which is divine and perfect in all of us." *

I accepted the invite and between half snow, half rain, and a chilly fog, arrived late. The small room was already filled with two handfuls of people--silent, peaceful, eyes closed. I felt like an intruder, but Sandra immediately changed that, graciously welcoming me and guiding me to a spot. She continued the meditation, moving sequentially from chakra to chakra, explaining the power and color of each. Colors we contain. Colors, like the sky--cool, fire, glowing, iridescent, morning, evening, cloudy, colors. As she spoke, I envisioned Kathy's Spirited Trees wooden planks and realized that if they were stacked one on top of the other, they would be hauntingly similar to the chakra colors aligned in our spines.

Sandra's voice was soothing, with a hint of spunk and a taste of a Spanish accent. She laughed easily and smiled generously. I attended that one session in March, but her energy and voice stayed with me. I want to know her whole story so seven months later, following an intuitive hit, I sent her an email. She replied immediately and opened her Sacred Doors once again. When I walked through, she gave me a hospitable hug, looked into my eyes and said, "I remember you."

---

* *"Sacred Doors Home Page." Accessed January 26, 2012., www.sacreddoors.net*

Sandra's stature is small and she radiates a very peaceful presence. We sit down, but before she begins to recount her story, she wants to see the Spirited Trees artwork. I take her to Kathy's website and she lets out a gasp, "Beautiful! This artist understands." I can tell from watching Sandra's eyes connecting with Kathy's pieces, she is someone who also understands.

Born in El Salvador (the country of the Savior), in a town named Alegria (which means happiness), Sandra lived in a tightly-knit community, her family at its center. Her grandmother, Maria Elena, a businesswoman who would seal deals with a firm handshake, started a grain mill and owned and rented land for growing corn and coffee beans while raising thirteen children. As her grandmother earned more and more money, she opened cantinas (little town bars) where people would gather to share news, drinks, stories, and songs. Sandra's mother, also named Maria Elena, was a powerful woman who earned a degree in teaching and social services and devoted her life to helping others find their true path.

As a child, Sandra would escape to the fruit groves and fall asleep in limbs under the protective canopies of citrus, mango, avocado, and eucalyptus trees. Here, she would dream, dream that she lived in trees, under the shade and in the light. I too remember my protective tree, a blood orange one, which grew at the edge of the retaining wall at my grandparents' home in Rose, Italy. I have never found a blood orange that can even come close to the ones that came from that tree--never. Rolling hills of fig and olive trees surrounded my grandparents' home, so delicious, so sweet. These hills would carry my grandmother's musical voice with news of births, deaths, sickness, recovery, work, scandal, and love. This is how the town would receive the news--through the transportive voices of women laboring in the fields. Stronger than steel wires, their voices traveled through the air and echoed in the trees. There are ancient memories in trees. Ancient memories that Sandra shares with me today.

Sandra:

"The scent of eucalyptus still reminds me of when my mother used to bathe me as a little girl, sprinkling eucalyptus leaves in the water. It was so soothing. I never, ever dared to climb cocoa trees because we have deep respect for them. To the Mayans, cocoa is a delectable food given to humans as a gift from the gods. There was also a rubber tree near my home and I would playfully poke at its bark until a white, sappy liquid would drip down. 'Stop!' my grandmother would beg. 'You're making the tree bleed!' I obeyed and immediately stopped poking the tree."

> For in truth, it is life that gives unto life while you, who deem yourself a giver, are but a witness.
>
> ~Kahlil Gibran

In the 1960s and 1970s, El Salvador, like most of Central America, became entrenched in civil war, revolution, and bloodshed. There was no middle class and no middle ground, just a few wealthy families who owned lots of land and the remaining population, the poor class, who owned nothing.

Sandra:

"Driving through the countryside, the horror of war came to life. I saw decapitated bodies hanging from trees with the heads propped up on fence spikes, blood dripping into the soil. War is ugly. It cannot be painted pretty. Fearing the guerilla soldiers would come, I would ask myself, 'Who will come in the night? Will I die tonight? Who will give me a proper burial?' I feared becoming a victim of war. But we escaped alive, my mother, brother, and me. We moved to the United States. I did not feel comfortable when I arrived. But I was happy, happy to be alive. Many years later, I went back to a destroyed country. I did not recognize it. There was no natural order, just complete destruction. The Salvadorian people are resilient, but traumatized. The community is broken. The youth absorbed anger, violence, and hatred. They were born in bloodshed and sadly, these victims often grow up victimizing others. They created gangs, some of which have become the most dangerous in the world. This is the result of war. So much ugliness."

Though raised as a Catholic and having grown up in a spiritual family, Sandra felt empty and cold from the ravages of war when she first moved to the United States. She began reading books on existentialism to uncover the meaning of her life. Even though she no longer practices her religion, she draws comfort from having learned there is only one light, one love, one being, one universal God. After some key events that offered new perspectives, Sandra shares how dramatically her life changed.

Sandra:
"My husband and I had been in business together for several years and even though we were financially successful, our marriage was no longer working. Twenty-five years of marriage and then it was finished. I was on vacation at a beautiful resort when I realized that having money and status do not define who we are. This is how it used to be: I would travel from my work in New York City to my home in Westport, exhausted, shuffling my feet on the train platform like a walking corpse. I was absolutely exhausted and then I would make dinner for my family. I did this every night, year after year. As a mother, I wanted to take care of my family. I also wanted a career, but not that way. Not with all of that aching. I ache when I see the epidemic of people disconnecting everywhere, cutting themselves off from their true self and from nature. I ache when I see trees being unnecessarily cut, trees that have lived for hundreds of years. My dream was to open a place of healing so that I could help others reconnect to themselves,

to nature, to wholeness. To stop the cutting and the aching."

In April of 2009, Sandra achieved her dream by opening Sacred Doors and bringing together an impressive consortium of acupuncturists, nutritionists, Reiki masters, and many other integrative counselors dedicated to helping individuals get on the road to health and healing. Traveling extensively to China, Japan, India, Thailand, Malaysia, The Philippines, all over Europe, and South and North America to meet with Buddhist masters, Sandra also had an opportunity to bask in the light of the Dalai Lama's presence. Attending a sangha (Sanskrit for: assembly with a common goal) in New York City's Radio City Music Hall, Sandra shares what it was like to be with the Dalai Lama.

> *Whatever a man offers me with true devotion, a leaf, a flower, fruit, water, I will accept it because it represents his heart's dedication.*
>
> *~Krishna*

Sandra:
"It was intellectual and complex and so beautiful to be with him, to get to see and feel him. He spoke about ancient scripture, but he started the lecture in layman's terms with a simple story. The Dalai Lama had been invited to India to be with Zen masters. They gathered and sat in a circle. One master arrived naked and the Dalai Lama, who was sitting next to him, put his hand on his knee and said, 'I really admire you. You're a man who doesn't hide anything.' The assembly roared in laughter."

Sandra laughs as she shares this with me and I laugh right along with her. After so much time, we can still laugh with those who have laughed before us.

Sandra is closely connected to the International Council of Thirteen Indigenous Grandmothers and is committed to carrying out the Council's mission of peace through sustainability. These grandmothers, who come from Alaska, Asia, Africa, and North, South, and Central America, formed a global alliance of healing, peace, and prayer from which to pass ancient seeds of knowledge to the next seven generations. The "seventh generation principle" is a law of sustainability established by the Iroquois Tribe, which urges people to think, decide, and act in ways that take into consideration the next seven future generations. "Look and listen for the welfare of the whole people and have always in view not only the present but also the coming generations, even those whose faces are yet beneath the surface of the ground – the unborn of the future Nation."*

As my time with Sandra is coming to a close, she shares some parting advice for moving towards enlightenment.

Sandra:
"Eat less meat. Learn to breathe. Practice kindness and compassion every day. And remember, flowers are the heart of a tree or a plant. They offer the strongest vibrations and make you remember you are a divine being. Spend some quiet time with flowers."

*"The Constitution of the Iroquois Nations." Accessed January 26, 2012., http://www.indigenouspeople.net/iroqcon.htm

RECEIVING

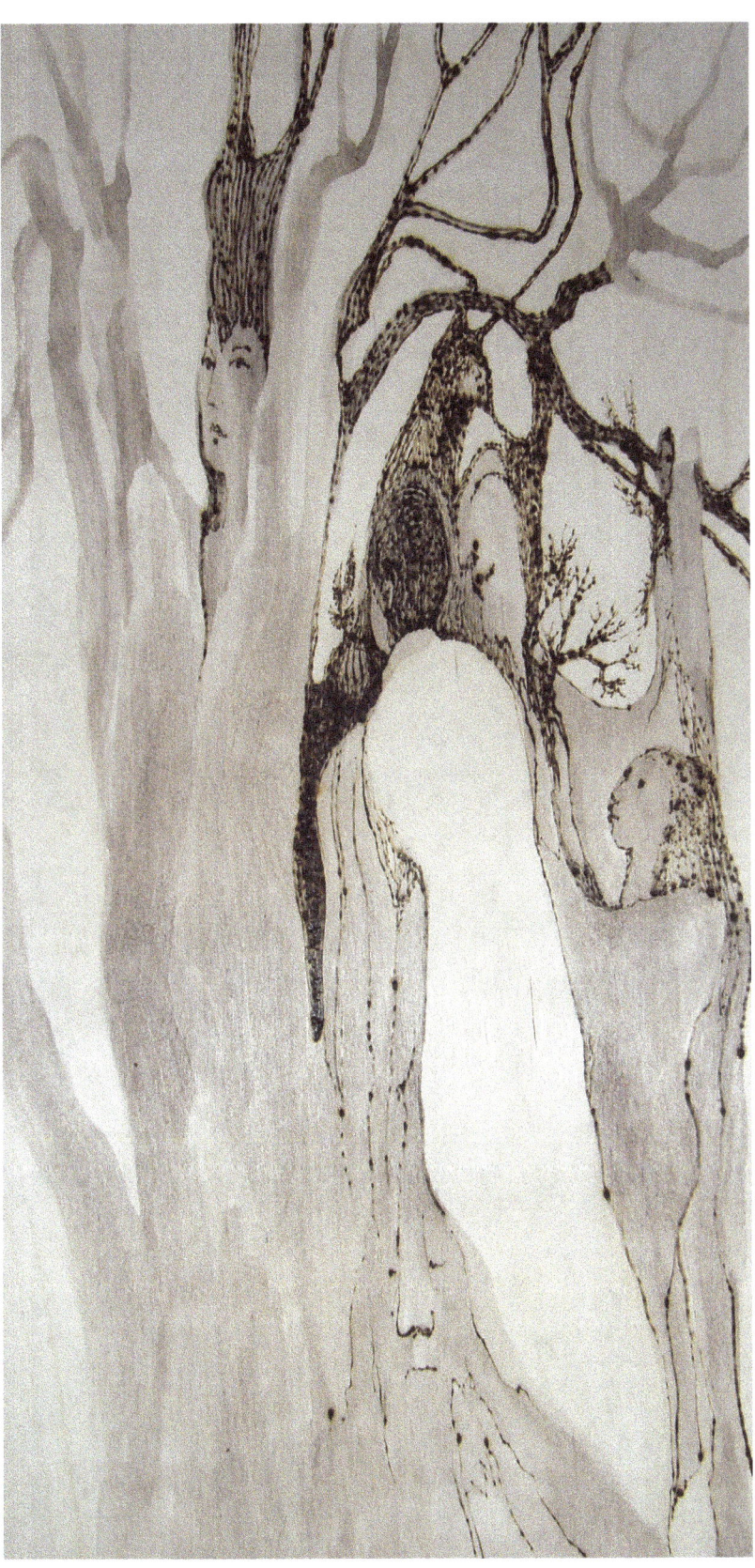

RECEIVING

Q: Do you receive in grace?
A: _____

From the heavens, lightning strikes,
Clashing clouds are round with light
Flashing fast cross a black, blustery night
A kindling scent fills the air and raining sky.

Raised from empyrean dust
And through a whispering breath,
We are perfect: half heaven, half earth
Cosmic bodies revolving, around a benevolent sun.

On this journey we seek the truth, and completely trust,
That in the act of offering, we too, will receive much wealth.
Through simple acts of simple kindness,
Gratitude, love, and grace, will drape in a clean white dress.

Waiting to return, to the place it all began,
Still deepening our roots and continuing our growth,
Anchored by the wisdom, of an elder, faceless sage,
The mystery of life emerges, from the fair Receiving tree.

Arcane divine forces, of ancient fire and water,
Moving fervently together, consuming and cleansing,
Secretly revealing, who we really are,
By balancing these gestures, of gracious giving and receiving.

K. Patricia Thrane

I met Patricia Thrane at St. John's rectory. She had come with Emilio Funicella to speak to The Flock young adult group about volunteer opportunities. Patricia is also a gardener who sometimes helps Emilio transport men from Liberation House to plant trees and flower beds at various places in Stamford. At the end of the evening, I introduced myself to Patricia and she shared that she is also an artist, photographer, and writer. In our short exchange, I could tell there was so much bubbling up in Patricia—so much passion, so much love, so much heart.

I thought of Patricia soon after our meeting. I was working on a story for *ARTES Magazine* about Partners for Architecture, a Stamford-based architectural firm that had collaborated with UNICEF on a project to build schools in Africa. The images the architects had available were computer renderings that lacked a sense of life. Because Patricia had traveled extensively through South Africa in the 1980s photographing apartheid and daily life in remote villages, I thought she might have some real photographs that could complement the story. It was as if I had met Patricia at exactly the right time to connect her art with a story because indeed she had many photographs and was happy to share them. Her photos of straw-thatched roofs and indigo ceiling tapestries added glimpses of the wonderful earth colors used in African architecture. I was so grateful to have these stark and very real images complementing the piece.

A year later, when I interviewed Emilio he said, "I know someone you should talk to for your book. She's amazing." As soon as he said this, I remembered Patricia and decided to contact her again.

I meet Patricia at her beautiful Colonial house, a house that has been in her family since 1965 and where she spent most of her childhood and teenage years. Patricia welcomes me at the massive, oak back door. As she holds it open, I notice her strong hands. They are almost manly, but Patricia is anything but. Statuesque, yes, but her fair complexion and green eyes are gentle and warm. She leads me into the kitchen to show me a statue of a Christ figure walking on water she is restoring, whose hands she is re-creating from scratch. The smell of plaster and coffee brewing feel oddly pleasant together.

> Forgiveness is the giving, and so the receiving of life.
>
> ~George MacDonald

We settle into the living room on a comfortable couch, the late morning winter sun streaming in. White light dances a top of the books, vases, photos, paintings, and even the piano. Patricia starts off softly, almost in a whisper, and shares that no matter what she is doing, her work is always about love. Even when it comes to butterflies.

Patricia:
"Monarch butterflies are an amazing species because they migrate thousands and thousands of miles every year to escape cold temperatures and to ensure that a new generation of monarchs will survive. It takes several generations to complete the migration. At each leg of the journey, the female monarchs lay eggs on milkweed so that the next generation can continue onto the next flight. Their antennae act like compasses and can detect a magnetic pull towards the light. They migrate to Mexico and cling to fir trees, completely covering the tree like a vine. Monarchs are becoming endangered for several reasons. One, with global warming, they are confused as to when the temperatures will cool. If they stay north longer, they literally risk being frozen to

death. And two, both here and in Mexico, their native micro-environments are being destroyed due to urbanization and deforestation. Butterflies need to lay their eggs on specific host plant species like milkweed, which they need to survive. Because there is an inter-connectedness in biodiversity and because butterflies are a keystone species, if we lose that which is such an important piece of the puzzle, we risk collapsing the whole ecosystem."

Like most of us, the visual beauty of butterflies charms Patricia. But as an artist and a gardener, she actively tries to preserve their natural and delicate habitats and encourages others to plant native species. Ten thousand milkweed patches would need to be planted every year to make up for the monarchs' habitat loss. She is working on having plant name tags commercially made so that the public becomes aware of the best varieties to plant. Patricia takes a hands-on approach when becoming involved in a cause. But first, she had to learn to "really see".

Patricia:
"There are two types of people in the world, those who enjoy being involved because they are aware of the world outside of themselves, and those who haven't learned to "really see". I was fortunate to learn to really see because my mother always encouraged me to experience the world. My family is Scottish and Norwegian and it felt very natural to travel back and forth between these two worlds. We grew up in this home in Greenwich, but when it was time to go to college, I wanted more than just a party scene filled with drugs, sex, and alcohol. In Europe, young people were more interested in talking about politics, so I chose to go to school in England. I was in a bookstore one day and picked up a book by Edvard Munch. That was the day I fell in love with art. When I was in school as a child, I would daydream looking out the window. And then when I was at home, I would spend hours staring at the

art on the walls. When I was eleven, my brother became a school photographer and I that's when I started to work in photography. Fascinated by the process, I spent hours working in a dark room. I became so immersed in

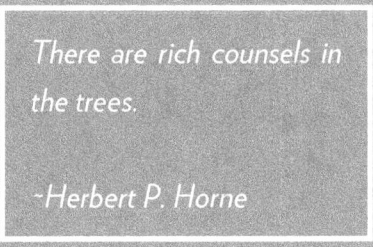

There are rich counsels in the trees.

-Herbert P. Horne

my own creative world, but I also stayed in tune with what was going on around the world. Sometimes it was through the dark room that I began seeing the world around me. I remember when a terrorist group attacked a marine base in 1983 and being moved by so many political events that seemed to be happening all at once. Seeing those images was moving and unsettling; I couldn't sit still in class. I was very affected by the violence and felt like I needed to help. My life seemed to support this urgent desire—I was not accepted into art school right away, which in retrospect opened the door to my going out into the world and really getting involved. I visited Cambodian refugee camps and went on a search to find a Thai general so that I could get permission to teach art to the children. I literally knocked on doors trying to find him and I did. I asked, and remarkably, he said yes. I remember one morning when we were sitting in a circle making art. The children were so intensely interested, surrounding me so tightly I could barely breathe. Bombs were falling around us and here we were making art. As the bombs came closer to the camp, we were told to leave, but I said no. I stayed with a doctor to help everyone evacuate. I was concerned that they were in serious danger and that no one would care. The truth is, I had fallen in love with these people so I was not about to abandon them. The art that came out of the children was unreal – planes, bombs, bloodshed. When it became too dangerous, I was forced to leave, but I didn't forget. That experience urged me to do more."

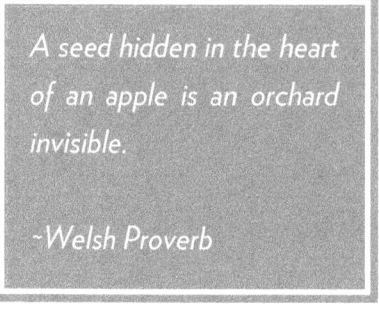

A seed hidden in the heart of an apple is an orchard invisible.

~Welsh Proverb

Breaking from the intensity of these memories, Patricia returns to happier ones from her childhood. Her mother and stepfather were great gardeners. They were always in nature and beautiful landscapes, nibbling blueberries right from bushes. She learned her awareness and appreciation from them. Her father died when she was three years old and she remembers her mother planting a tree in his honor. As Patricia grew, she would sometimes ask her mother where her father was and her mother would point to the tree and say that the ambulance had climbed up the tree and taken him to heaven. "As a child, I always wanted to climb that tree," she says.

Patricia:
"After my father passed away, my mother took over the family finances. She became a savvy investor. Seeing her do this made me realize that I could also take control of my finances. I never really had an interest in the financial world, but just like I invest my time in people and projects, my financial resources need to be spent well, and I realized I can have a say in this. My father had worked on Wall Street and was well-regarded all over the world. My memories of my father are faint, but I hold on to them dearly. I remember him through stories that my mother told me. My stepfather was also an amazing person. He was a world-renowned hematologist but he was also so humble and down to earth. He was a handyman type, always fixing something around the house. When everyone thought I was lost, traveling the world and creating art, he told me I was on the right path. I was fortunate to be surrounded by such nurturing people growing up. As I experienced more and more of the world, even at such devastating levels of war

and poverty, I felt hopeful. When I was in my early twenties, I was in Paris and met Dali Tambo, the son of Oliver Tambo who was president of the African National Congress and founder of Artists Against Apartheid in London. We would spend hours talking politics and art; I fell in love. It was truly love at first sight. We became a team working on many projects together. Dali is the one who led me to live and work in South Africa in the mid-1980s. I pretended to be a fashion photographer but was really there to photograph migrant labor camps and the poverty. It was difficult working in secret and I ended up being caught and arrested. It sounds very dramatic, but luckily, I was able to hand over my camera to a colleague and they never found the seven rolls of film I had on me! I was meeting so many talented people who were full of fire and wanted to make life peaceful. I met Jonas Gwangwa, who is a phenomenal South African jazz musician. We worked together on concerts sponsored by Artists Against Apartheid, including the "Nelson Mandela 70th Birthday Tribute" in 1988, part of the campaign for Mandela's release from prison. Music has an immediate effect on moving people."

Patricia is filled with joie de vivre--loving life and living in love. I wonder what happened to the love she had with Dali and she tells me distance separated it. She had to move back to the United States, but they remain close friends and sometimes collaborate on projects together. For a moment, Patricia grows still and quiet. Then she begins to tell me about her failed marriage, her voice low and raspy. "It seemed perfect," she says. "He was an ivy-league graduate, well respected, and well-to-do. But our home became another battlefront of emotional and physical abuse."

I am surprised, but not really. It is easy to take advantage of a generous person's compassion. Generosity can be abused. Traumatized by the abuse, Patricia does not remember many details, but as she puts her hands up to her neck and her eyes begin to water, she shares this in a voice that is barely a whisper.

Patricia:
"He tried to take away my voice. I didn't deserve this. I had protected so many people and their rights, now I had to fight for mine. In 2004, I was asked to speak at a UNESCO event at the University of Connecticut on rights and peace. Ironically, I thought I don't have the qualifications to talk about this. I didn't want to do it, but they encouraged me so I did and it was empowering to release my voice to others. War is ugly but it can also make people gentle. We become more intellectually and emotionally developed through empathy. Everything I do-- the art I create, the gardens I plant--are out of my love for people. We can be a voice for each other. Who will be a voice for nature?"

LISTENING

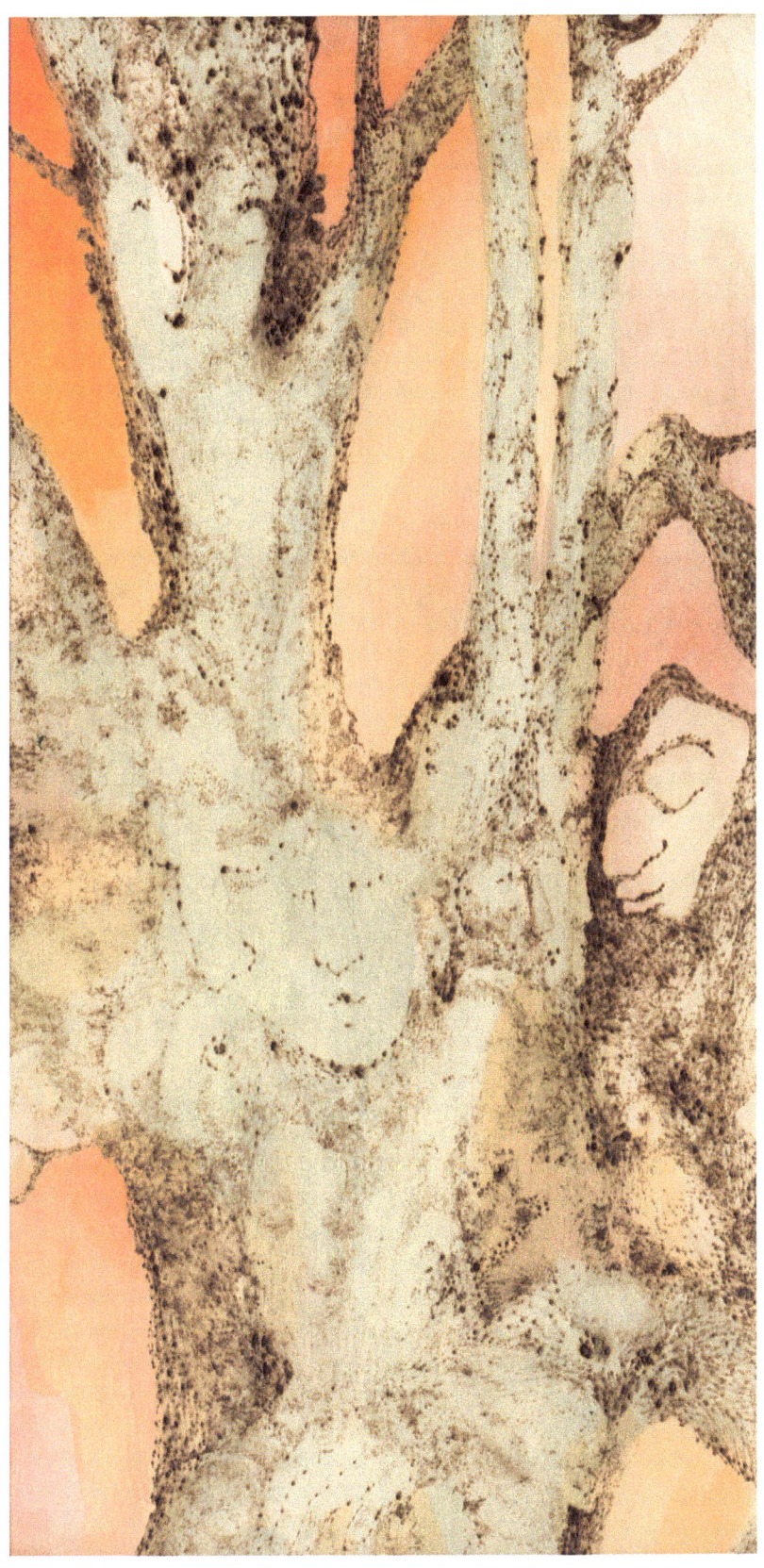

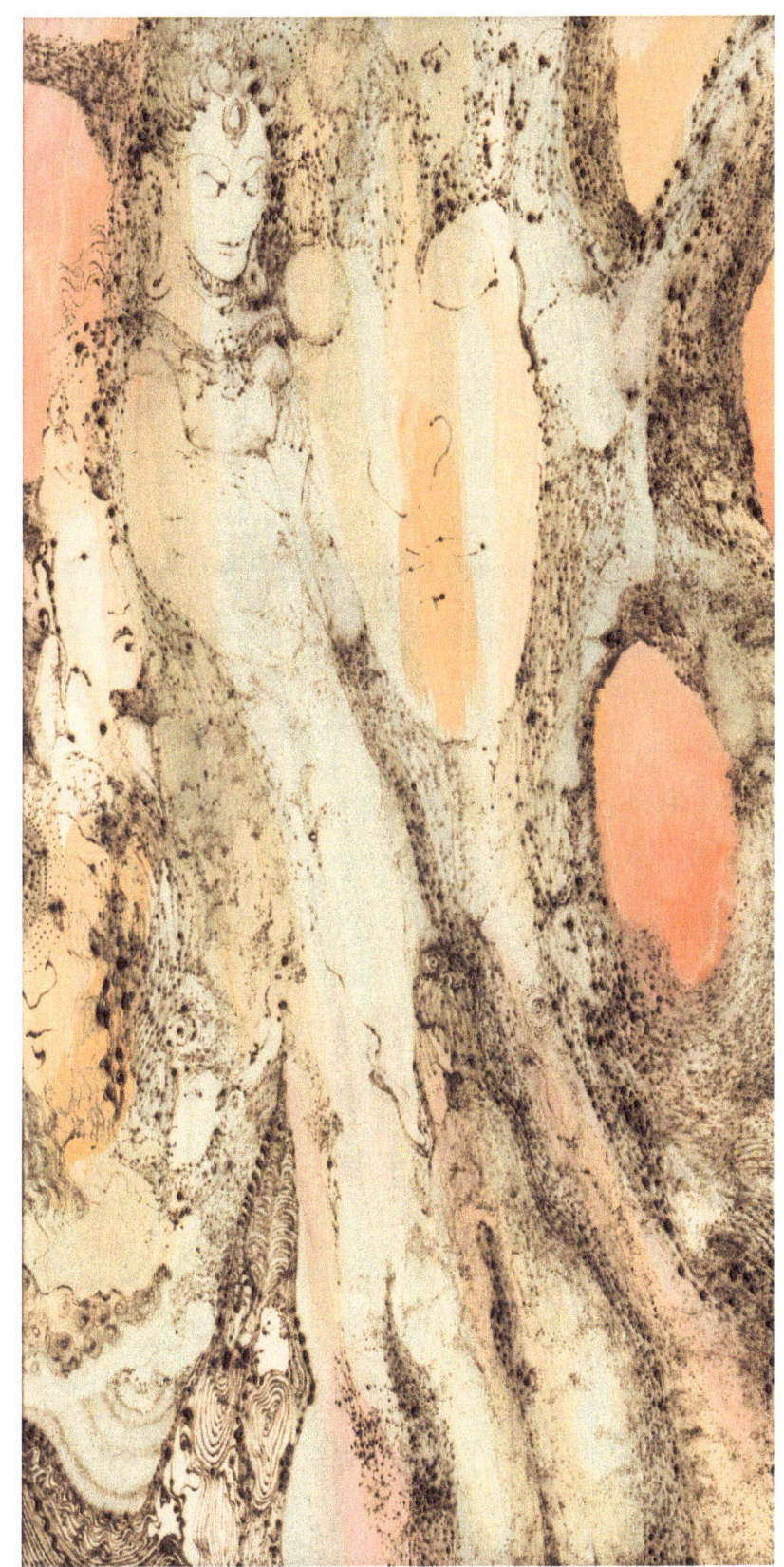

LISTENING

Q: Do you hear your heart?
A: _____

A stream of outside sounds surrounds us:
Whispering winds, lapping waves,
Clapping hands, crying babes,
Pacing steps, swinging doors,

Humming machines, constant chatter,
Blaring traffic and ticking clocks.
Loud noise creates louder talk,
Our place is lost, the meaning--gone.

We hear half the story, its message warped,
Until silence breaks and opens the heart,
To listen beyond the spoken words,
Connected, sentient, at a higher level.

Entering inside, we find secret notes,
Of the dulcet harmony in nature:
A sparrow's song, a butterfly's flap, bees buzzing in a spreading
meadow
Expressing emotions in pitch-perfect code.

This is how beauty speaks with urgency,
In an orange sky--quiet dawn, quiet dusk
Listening with eyes wide shut,
In holes and valleys that echo: Listen to me!

Susan Freeland

As I sat and talked with Sandra Angulo at Sacred Doors—a healing and education center in Norwalk, Connecticut that teaches body, mind, spirit connectedness and wholeness—Susan Freeland walked in. Sandra introduced us and when Susan said hello, her voice sounded like a deliciously slow spoonful of honey. Susan is a licensed Zyto EVOX practitioner a.k.a. voice mapping therapist, which is someone who studies underlying tones in a person's voice and traces emotional and behavioral patterns connected to them. I am fascinated by Susan and her work, so at the end of Sandra's interview, we scheduled a time to meet. This is how I met Susan, synchronistically, as she walked through Sacred Doors.

Susan cleared her afternoon for me, even though I told her the interview would only take about an hour. Feeling anxious, I start to wonder what she will hear in my voice. Will she pick up on something I am not aware of? What answers will she find in my questions? As the time draws near, I become more and more conscious of my quiet voice and loud laugh. Even though I am the one interviewing her, I feel as if she will be the one truly listening.

When we meet, there is no movement in her office, just silence. And then, as if on a conductor's cue, our two voices begin. Before delving into Susan's background, she opens the conversation with a statement so simple and profound, "Nature comes to help you."

I hear this and ponder its profound truth. How often do we think of nature, the environment, and planet earth as obligations or burdens? They are more things to care for on an already too long list. Every day we see reminders to pick up litter, don't pollute, recycle this, recycle that, eat organic, buy local...on and on and on. There are so many things to remember and do that it is sometimes easier to just ignore it all, rationalizing that we don't have the time, or worse, that we just don't care. We have a choice to care; nature does not.

It is said that nature can heal itself. Yes, to a certain degree, this is true. But sometimes people use this excuse to justify behavior that is harmful to the environment and to others. What about when we get sick, do we say, "I'll heal myself"? Sure, we can cure a cold with chicken soup and green tea. But what about when we are very ill and need real help? That's when we seek expert advice. Nature is like this: It seems to find us when we need it most.

Susan:
"My home backs up to a nature preserve where there is a divine canopy of trees that I can walk under anytime. I am so lucky; I get to see and hear nature calling every day, from the moment I awake until the moment my head hits the pillow and sometimes, even in my dreams. One night, a coyote howled mournfully at the moon, echoing into the darkness. Another night, an owl sat cozily in a tree, flew off, came back, sat again, stared at me, and flew off a second time. There are so many joyful little squirrels scurrying up trees and hanging by their tails. It's like they are putting on a special show just for me. My bedroom window is level with the tree canopy, so I feel like a bird in a nest in my own home. For many, many years I lived, or rather did not live, while working in Chicago as a mortgage financial consultant. I began seeing unscrupulous situations that I chose not to participate in. Long before the recession, I saw how people were being taken advantage of. They were buying themselves into bad situations they thought were good, but in the end, they could not buy themselves out. I was exhausted, sick, and had no life. Every day I

> *Use what talents you possess: the woods would be very silent if no birds sang there except those that sang best.*
>
> ~Henry Van Dyke

worked like a machine, punching numbers— real, imaginary, unreal, contrived numbers. I felt enslaved to a system that blocked any quality of life. Then one morning I had an epiphany: The stock market was indeed a bullpen of furious energy that I needed to escape alive. This was supposed to be the place where we put our trust, our hope for the future, and here it was collapsing right before me. We should plan for our future, but what about now? What do we hope for today? What can we build that won't collapse? And the only answer is ourselves. We can build ourselves. We are a complex system with simple needs. It's a broad statement to make, but we have focused so much on material needs that we've ended up cutting off vital spiritual and energetic flows, which make us feel like we have a life worth living. Ultimately, what we seek is love. I was married, but there wasn't any love. My husband committed a betrayal of the heart and at the time, I almost felt as if I deserved it. But my belief system changed. I realized I didn't need to stay with someone forever to be happy. I was already with someone and not happy. It was empowering to let go of everything, especially my marriage because it had become so unhealthy. I believe if you let go of something that is not making you happy, you make room for something greater. I still have respect for my former husband because negativity and his betrayal are not the whole truth. When we hurt, we feed ourselves negativity and lies because we think this will make us feel better. In reality, we have lost the ability to nurture ourselves like the way a tree instinctually knows how to nurture itself. Yes, we have to mourn our losses and mend our sorrows, but then we have to allow the light to enter. When I was going through my divorce, I learned that the courtroom is actually a place where people act out their unresolved conflicts and childhood traumas. For me, it was the place where my inability to speak up really became apparent. I literally had no voice. But even though I could not utter what I was feeling, I began to really hear the inner voice of my own heart."

Leaving her old life behind, Susan moved to Connecticut and began putting her nurturing efforts into helping adults and children. In 2007, she became an elementary school, special education paraprofessional. But here again she noticed that something was off. The prescribed, regimented education system was hindering the spirit of children rather than honoring their greatness. She would hear fear in their voices, a sound that was very familiar to her, and realized she wanted to help them see that there was absolutely nothing to be afraid of, that they are perfectly whole, loveable beings. Susan spent time with them, talked with them, listened to them, and came up with creative solutions to help eliminate their debilitating fear.

Susan clues me in to what caused her own debilitating fear by sharing her personal birth experience—she was brought into the world with forceps that left a scar on her skull and negatively affected her vision. Because of this, she internalized the belief that she was brought into the world as a damaged person, which then externalized as her voice literally getting stuck in her throat, as if she was being choked. As I hear the mellifluous and strong sound of her voice now, it is hard to imagine anything else.

Susan:
"Cells, which are the smallest structures that make up our bodies, absorb sounds and keep them locked in memory. When I started voice mapping for myself, I began to see so many truths laid out in front of me. I couldn't deny that the pain I felt was inside me. When I started to release conflicting

beliefs, my body began to heal. I realized conformity is not a safety zone. We can play many roles in life, but there is no need to wear a mask. The Zyto EVOX system that I use in my practice analyzes patterns, systems, and everything we have been taught to believe as children, which ends up being what we believe as adults. You speak into the system through a headphone on any topic you wish while placing your hand into a hand-cradle device. Your voice's energy is recorded through bio-communication and then plotted according to a Perception Index. I ask my patients questions to better understand their history and by using the Zyto EVOX system, I hear another layer to their answers, and can see not only how they perceive themselves, but also how their physical body responds to preferences. A circular map divided into twelve segments is produced and then color-coded. The twelve segments measure unacknowledged feelings versus self-validation, repetitive thinking versus creative thinking, depression versus inner peace, emotional disconnection versus emotional integration, rigid belief systems versus open possibilities, conditional love versus unconditional love, namely, everything we perceive ourselves to be. It is a powerful tool because we can actually see our voice. We can see the weakest link, and usually, in the weakest link we find the solution. We have twelve chords in our voice and there are twelve strands in our DNA. Without a full voice, we feel lost. Our nervous system is like a tree's root system; it carries everything it absorbs and then stores it in the brain, whether the thoughts and images are real or imagined."

Susan lets me experiment with voice mapping. Closing my eyes, I do not hear any external sounds. I begin repeating a phrase, one that seems to emerge from deep within myself. She plots my voice energy and I see stories that are like parts of me mapped in different colors. When I hear myself, even just repeating the phrase "listen to me" I hear others from my life too. I hear a quiet child's voice learning to speak. How the words come so easily for some and for others, they stumble. It is like tracing a family tree through your voice; oral histories passed down from generation to generation, somewhat in hieroglyphics. We collect so many stories from each other, cradling them in silence, even when we speak.

A bird does not sing because it has an answer. It sings because it has a song.

~Chinese Proverb

My time with Susan makes me feel completely open, even with so much to do, the busy-ness of the external world blurs into the background. She tells me listening is about being present in the day, today, not yesterday, or tomorrow. Listening is about letting go of anger and resentment and forgiving yourself and others so that you can finally be at peace. I listen to Susan's last story about a bird that made a nest near her front door right after she had moved into her new home.

Susan:
"Every day I would come home and check in on the nest to see if anything new had happened while I was away. Then one night, we had a storm with heavy rain and winds that knocked down the nest. All the eggs broke. The next morning, a flock of wren came to clean the nest. It was beautiful to see how communities in nature care for each other. Then, as the days

went by, I noticed that the bird started to rebuild its nest. It was amazing to see how even after being shattered, this little bird was able to put her life back together. Her new eggs hatched and the bird used her voice to attune her chicks and to ask a male bird to bring more food. So many lovely things happen in trees. There is deep meaning in the songs of birds."

ARRIVING

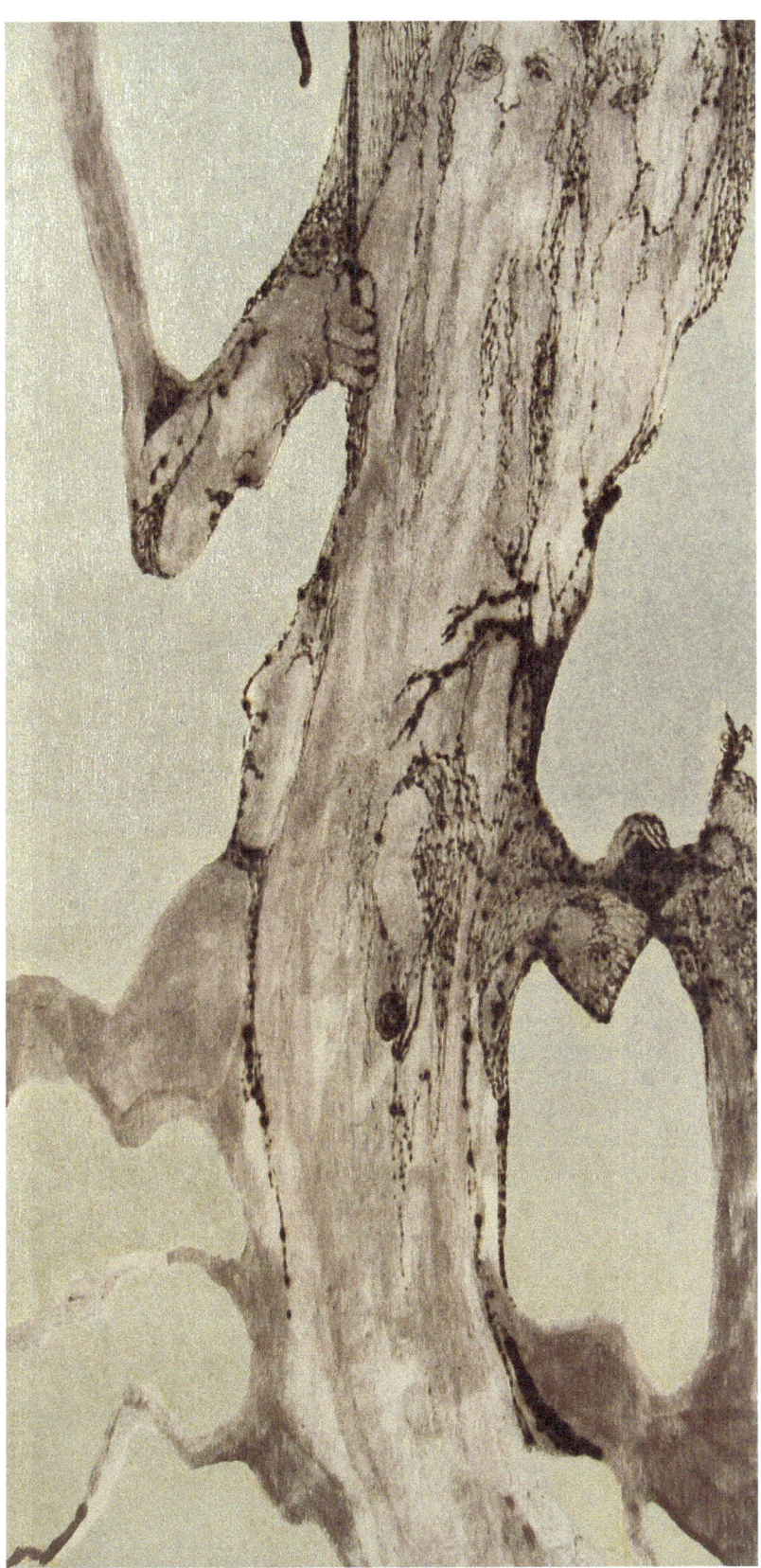

ARRIVING

Q: How do you arrive upon a question?
A: _____

Have you ever discovered an answer,
Only leads to more questions?
Arriving is beginning,
A place to stand and take a step further.

Leaving behind worn ways of thinking,
We leap with faith into unknown waters.
A point in time where awareness peaks,
A knock on the door, sshhh, someone is here.

Opening, arriving is to keep going,
To clear a path,
To live with purpose,
Never forgetting the past.

Arriving is time,
Patiently, quietly, waiting, time.
A circle, a ring, a point on a line,
Unexpectedly leading, unexpectedly following.

Paths cross, bells chime,
Wells dry up and overflow...
Shimmering in gold,
Arriving is seductive.

A time to wake to a new day and fall back to dream,
A time and space to travel and transport,
Figures move swiftly, slowly trotting towards wisdom,
And open a path to the summit atop

Where two wise men stand:
One, a pharaoh, shielded by falcon's wings,
The other, bearded, walking staff in hand,
He sees time. Arriving upon wisdom takes time.

Stephen Grasso & Rainer Schrom

In the fall of 2009, I attended a green lecture that was part of Stamford's SoundWater Lunch and Learn series. Steve Grasso and Rainer Schrom (co-principals of Partners for Architecture (PFA) and experts on sustainable building systems) were the guest speakers. As they spoke about blown cellulose insulation, renewable energy systems, vacuum glazing, rainwater harvesting, and solar heat powered cooling (topics that some might consider achingly dull), I noticed something in the room that I wasn't expecting—a completely captivated audience. The 100+ attendees were visibly enraptured by Steve and Rainer's passion, eagerly wanting to learn what they could do to become more sustainable in their own homes.

Several months later, I interviewed Steve and Rainer for an ARTES Magazine piece I was working on at their then newly renovated studio. Once a factory plant that manufactured shims for tanks during World War II, the studio's smaller conference room was formerly a vault that stored sensitive military papers. The original weathered brick walls now displayed the firm's drawing board sketches and construction documents, ranging from high-rises, to country clubs, to cultural art centers. The sleek workspace was a union of openness and light, allowing for a liberal exchange of ideas between the architects.

As we sat in the large conference room, warm light streamed on to the many project models and miniatures, including one of a school in the heart of the African jungle. By way of a highly competitive process, Steve and Rainer were selected by UNICEF (United Nations Children's Fund, a global steward of human rights for children) to create a master plan from which eighty schools

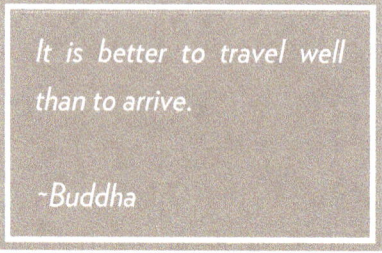

It is better to travel well than to arrive.

~Buddha

were to be built across the borders of four, civil war ravaged African countries: Republique de Guinea, Côte D'Ivoire, Liberia, and Sierra Leone.

After decades of war, these countries have finally begun to recover from a cataclysmic collapse of government, shelter, and education, and are shifting from a struggle-stricken state of mind to one of hopeful possibility. UNICEF has taken a leadership role in supporting this new way of thinking, especially when planning for educational safe havens through the LAB4LAB (Learning Along Borders for Living Across Boundaries) initiative. The program's objective is to provide safe, innovative learning environments with key community links that promote social activity. This, in turn, would stimulate sustainable economic development in these war torn countries, and would also serve as a successful model for future peace building interventions.

Though PFA accepted their assignment with gusto, it was a goal easier said than done. Though they faced many challenges along the way, they never lost sight of the vision and the team succeeded in translating a utopian concept into a real, physical solution over a period of three months.

Throughout the design phase, Carlos Vasquez, an architect from UNICEF's Education Section, facilitated communication between the African local communities and the architects in Connecticut. After meeting with Steve and Rainer, I contacted Carlos, and over a lunch of half-shell oysters, he shared his world travel experiences.

Carlos:
"It is critical to involve the local community from the very beginning in order to increase their vital ownership and

participation. Communities understand what their problems are with the land, the regional conditions, and the resources, or lack thereof. If they feel forced to use a space that is foreign to them, and implemented without taking their concerns into account, we run the risk that the schools will be rejected, underutilized, and possibly vandalized."

Steve and Rainer agreed with Carlos—dialogue with the local communities was key in planning the design. "We invited their opinions and needed their knowledge just as much as they wanted ours," said Steve. Even though the design work was prepared in the United States, UNICEF worked with local architects, engineers, and contractors in Africa, who were then able to explain the simple building method to the labor force during the construction phase. Carlos believes that this participation was crucial. First, it vitalized an economy in which there was a cash transfer for services. Second, there was a dissemination of technical knowledge and skills utilized in construction. By passing along this knowledge, the local communities would then be able to spread innovative design and construction practices, while at the same time develop independently.

Upon completion of the design phase, Carlos travelled to three of the four countries and presented the plans to government officials and the respective local communities. Locals performing traditional songs and dances, tears of joy streaming down their faces, welcomed Carlos with unbridled jubilation.

Carlos:
"Because many different dialects are spoken in Central Africa, I did not always understand what the people were saying, but the language of human emotion was more than evident. Village elders in Liberia arrived with two goats to show their gratitude. We graciously accepted the goats so that they would not feel offended. We packed the two goats into our compact car and after driving for more than three

hours to the next villages, and we gave the goats to locals who could undoubtedly make better use of them. Projects like the LAB4LAB initiative transcend cultural barriers and language. Seeing a community galvanize around a project offers hope that a new life can begin."

Designing schools in the heart of the Sub Saharan region presented many challenges. "Our sophisticated construction methods that involve machinery were simply not going to work," Rainer said. "With no running water, no sanitary system, no paved roads, and no electricity, we had to figure out a way to literally build with our hands."

PFA learned that African architecture tends to consist of adobe-walled structures and circular grass-thatched huts that effectively camouflage into the earth's color-rich landscape. Africans' lives revolve around this landscape and view architecture as shelter from the elements.

Taking all these factors into account, Steve and Rainer seized the opportunity, facing tremendous limitations that ironically offered them creative liberation. Effective design, as they had always known effective design to be, had to be thrown out and replaced with a new and revitalizing freedom to reinvent. Inspiration, they learned, comes from not having preconceived notions.

Delving into the diverse history, culture, and geography of these African countries, PFA learned that even though war had broken the land and their spirits, awareness that their small tribe was part of a larger world still existed. After centuries of colonialism, and a history riddled with poverty and war, African religion, politics, economics, and architecture have succumbed to western and eastern influences. But the most heartbreaking devastation has occurred as a result of the recent civil war, a conflict that has created tension between brothers, alienated neighboring countries, and left millions of indigenous people uprooted and oppressed. Diverse landscapes of tropical rainforests, open grass plains, and thick mangroves have been destroyed by the paramilitary groups' slash and burn practices. Once a territory rich in diamonds, gold, iron ore, cocoa, and coffee, these countries' have been mined, exploited, and left barren for the benefit of a few. Steve's perspective on this severe land pillaging cuts right to the heart of the matter, "There are two groups of people in the world those that are oppressed and those that oppress."

> *A good traveler has no fixed plans, and is not intent on arriving.*
>
> *-Lao Tzu*

PFA's role in designing the school master plans was to assist UNICEF in lifting the oppression, thereby aiding the oppressed. "We are a company comprised of architects with very diverse backgrounds and we like to believe that how we design and how we comport ourselves in the world creates positive cultural effects," continued Steve. "We realize our actions and the choices we make have consequences, not only on the local natural environment, but on the global psychological landscape as well."

PFA rejected a preliminary site plan that would have required the burning and clearing of trees, standing firm that they would not contribute to a design that encouraged further deforestation and environmental degradation. Instead, they developed a model that mimicked a beehive form of hexagonal shaped pods dispersed between the trees. Connecting the pods allowed for flexibility at different locations and expandability to accommodate a future surge of students.

Rainer:
"Safety was a critical design issue we had to consider, so we designed pods that consisted of three sections. The first

access area is the most publicly used space. Then, moving in towards the center, are the school administrative offices and computer labs. And finally, going in deeper, are private classrooms where the youngest group of children are sheltered in the innermost circular space. Africans tend to teach their children in circles rather than rows, so our design supported what they were already comfortable with. The hexagon shape leaves an opportunity to build community, share borders, and promote a democratic participation."

All the hallways are open-air exterior spaces. The building materials are native wood, metal, and adobe. The roofs are solar power ready so that panels can be installed and wired to provide electricity for the computer lab. Rather than covering the classroom ceilings with a metal roof, PFA proposed incorporating vibrantly colored hand-woven African fabrics strewn over the rafters that evoke heritage and history.

In addition to the physical structure and aesthetics, PFA strategized how the buildings would function. As there was no running water or sanitary sewer system available, dry latrines located in dark interior spaces were proposed to help avoid the spread of disease. Screen covered chimneys would be set up to allow for natural light and for preventing an onslaught of flies from penetrating. Human waste could then be collected, composted, and used as fertilizer to re-introduce nutrients into the soil. In its most basic sense, even the latrine system design is one that would give back and make the soil fertile again.

Rainer:
"As architects, we believe that positive buildings in communities won't be vandalized if their function is clear. We find satisfaction in designing public buildings because they have a larger impact on community and society. In our corner of the world, property and real estate value are most

important, with people building and living in their homes always cognizant of a future sale. A home should be an investment in life rather than the market. Every day is a struggle to find a meeting place of cultural differences between luxury and necessity. We think where the sun meets the horizon is our common ground."

Construction of the schools began in February 2009 and continues to progress, even though funding has declined due to current global economic conditions. Far from reaching the construction of all eighty schools, UNICEF is in the process of working towards achieving its goal of providing low carbon footprint schools and universal access to education for all children. One school in Ganta, Liberia has been totally completed, providing a safe haven of education for its children, and at the same time, an opportunity to promote peace, a process that never ceases. There are currently close to forty schools that have been implemented across borders.

The way PFA made saving the trees such an integral part of their school design has stayed in the forefront of my mind. I realized that by saving the trees, they saved a primal connection—the children to their communities, the communities to the earth, and finally, the earth back to the children.

> The nonviolent approach does not immediately change the heart of the oppressor. It first does something to the hearts of those committed to it. It gives them a new self-respect; it calls up resources of strength and courage that they did not know they had. Finally, it reaches the opponent and so stirs his conscience that reconciliation becomes reality.
>
> ~Martin Luther King, Jr.

In 2011, I contact them again to see if they would participate in the Spirited Trees project. As before, they are gracious and say yes. But this time, I request to interview them separately, to better understand who they are as individuals, to hear their own unique voices. I meet with Steve first and ask him to tell me more about the oppressed and oppressor theory.

Steve:
"With whom does one relate? Those who identify with the oppressed see justice. They have compassion for people who cannot help themselves. Maybe it's because they are not in the right circle to succeed, or they were never part of the "in" crowd, or they do not have the means or resources to break the cycle of a poverty mentality. I seem to find it easier to identify with the outsider. My grandparents were immigrants, so they were outsiders by nature. My parents were more settled and I am even more so because I am second generation. I am an American, but I still do not feel close enough to be completely American. I feel and live my roots. I grew up in the Bronx and Mount Vernon with a strong sense of family and in an Italian American community. I noticed that within the community where I lived, there were people who held prejudices, and I just couldn't understand why. And what was even more disturbing were those that held these negative beliefs toward outsiders had been the outsiders themselves, not that long ago. There was an influx of more immigrants and even though the communities grew in diversity, they also became more bigoted. Neighborhoods back then were structures of culture; they were live, breathing spaces with recognizable identities. There were friendly relationships between neighbors. Everyone knew and protected each other. Now, people who live right across the street from each other act like strangers. We don't take time to communicate with those who are in such close proximity. That safety network

is broken. As I grew up and met new people from different cultures, my own views began to change. I realized that you can never fully understand people and their realities until you open your mind."

Building a community is a state of mind just as much, if not more, than building physical roadways. Steve is active in raising a sustainable local community through his active leadership in Sustainable Stamford, a city task force that promotes green-minded events, projects, and programs to educate the public on sustainable living. He also brings a diverse mix of individuals together every month at Green Drinks events to share sustainable ideas. Steve believes, "by taking little steps to be green, people will feel that what they believe to be impossible is very possible."

Rainer agrees that by beginning with an idea, no matter how simple or grand, and then taking action, we can arrive at our goals. It may be a direct route of action or it may be a winding road, but the most important thing is to continue to depart and arrive again and again.

> Rainer:
> "I grew up a skeptic. I questioned everything. I was born in Germany, southern Bavaria, in a very Catholic and conservative area of the country. But my parents encouraged me to question, not simply to believe. I always felt a connection to nature. I remember my father wanted to cut down trees around the house because they had become overgrown. With tears rolling down my face, I begged him not to. The trees were so old; they had a right to remain there. I always loved climbing trees and enjoyed being in this elevated position because of the view. As an adult, this translated into having an expanded horizon beyond what we tend to keep ourselves locked into."

As Rainer describes the forest view of mottled greens, I remember a different one, of red rooftops, during my time in

> *What we call the beginning is often the end. And to make an end is to make a beginning. The end is where we start from.*
>
> *-T.S. Eliot*

Florence, Italy when I was studying abroad. One of the first things many students did when they arrived was to climb the tower of the Duomo. I was intrigued, I wanted to see the view but decided to wait. There were many days spent on lonely excursions traversing twisting cobblestone roads, which led me to unknown places. At that moment of panic, whenever I felt lost, I would look up to try to find a glimpse of the hovering dome to orient myself. It wasn't until my very last day in the city that I climbed to the top. Through the dark, winding staircases, the setting sun illuminated the next step for me as I peered through the punched out square windows in the massive stone walls, flashbacks of where I had been, like a city map. Then finally, out on the Duomo's balcony, was a city that I had discovered, a city that I could now read like the lines of my palm. I relished that moment—a pink December sky welcoming me at the end of my day, like I had just been awakened.

Rainer:
"As I grew older and studied architecture, I began to understand people. Creating spaces meant that I must place human beings in positions where they are conscious of their surroundings. I've been to Africa, traveled through the desert, came in close contact with the locals, and saw how they live and what they expect from their surroundings. It would have been wrong to design an American style school expecting the Africans to adapt to it. I call this compassionate design—to design for the needs of others, not for yourself or your ego. The human experience starts when we are infants, with our mothers and fathers giving us a sense of security and fulfilling all of our basic needs.

As we grow and have new experiences, we become more independent. When we designed the LAB4LAB school plan, PFA provided these basic needs too: a roof, safety, and nourishing light. But we didn't tell them how to decorate their interior space. How could I make that assumption? It would be so wrong to do that. Just a few months ago, I visited the Art Gallery of Ontario and saw an exhibit that featured slices of fallen tree trunks and found stumps. Some of the rings were small while others were enormous. The artist had removed a specific section of the tree that represented an exact time in that tree's life. That hollow portion made me think about what might have happened in the tree's history, about peeling back all the layers of a human being and discovering the child again."

CREATING

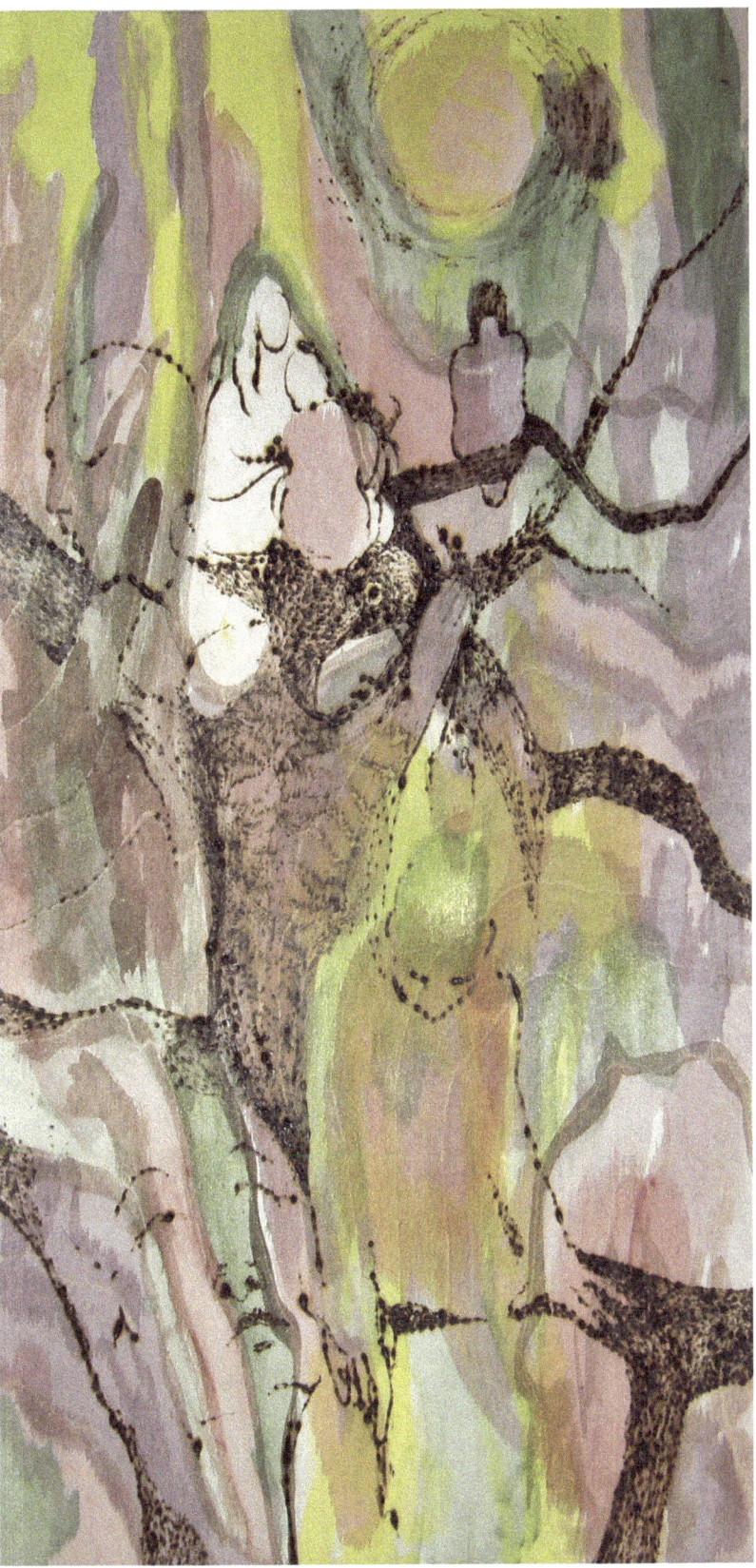

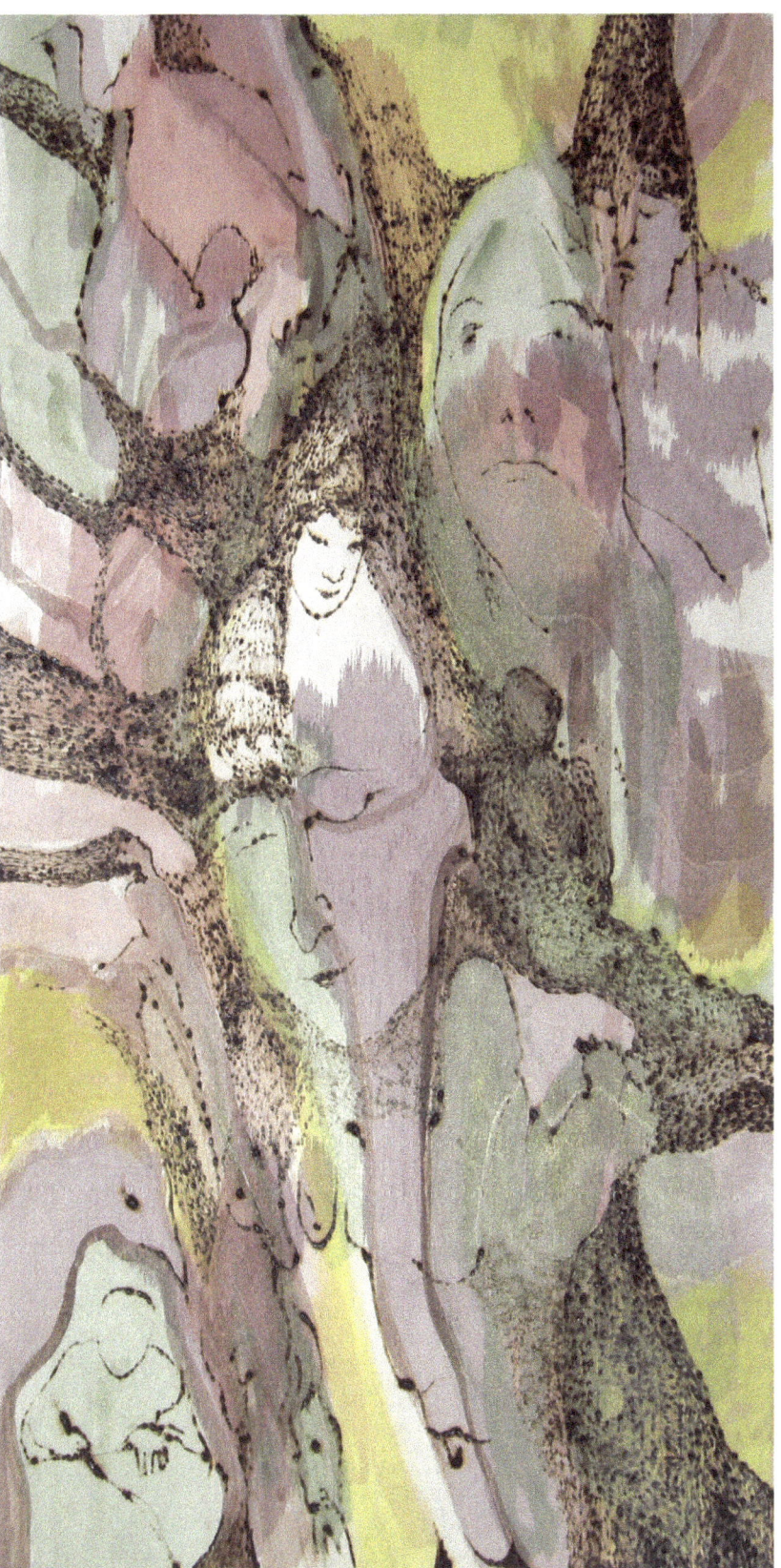

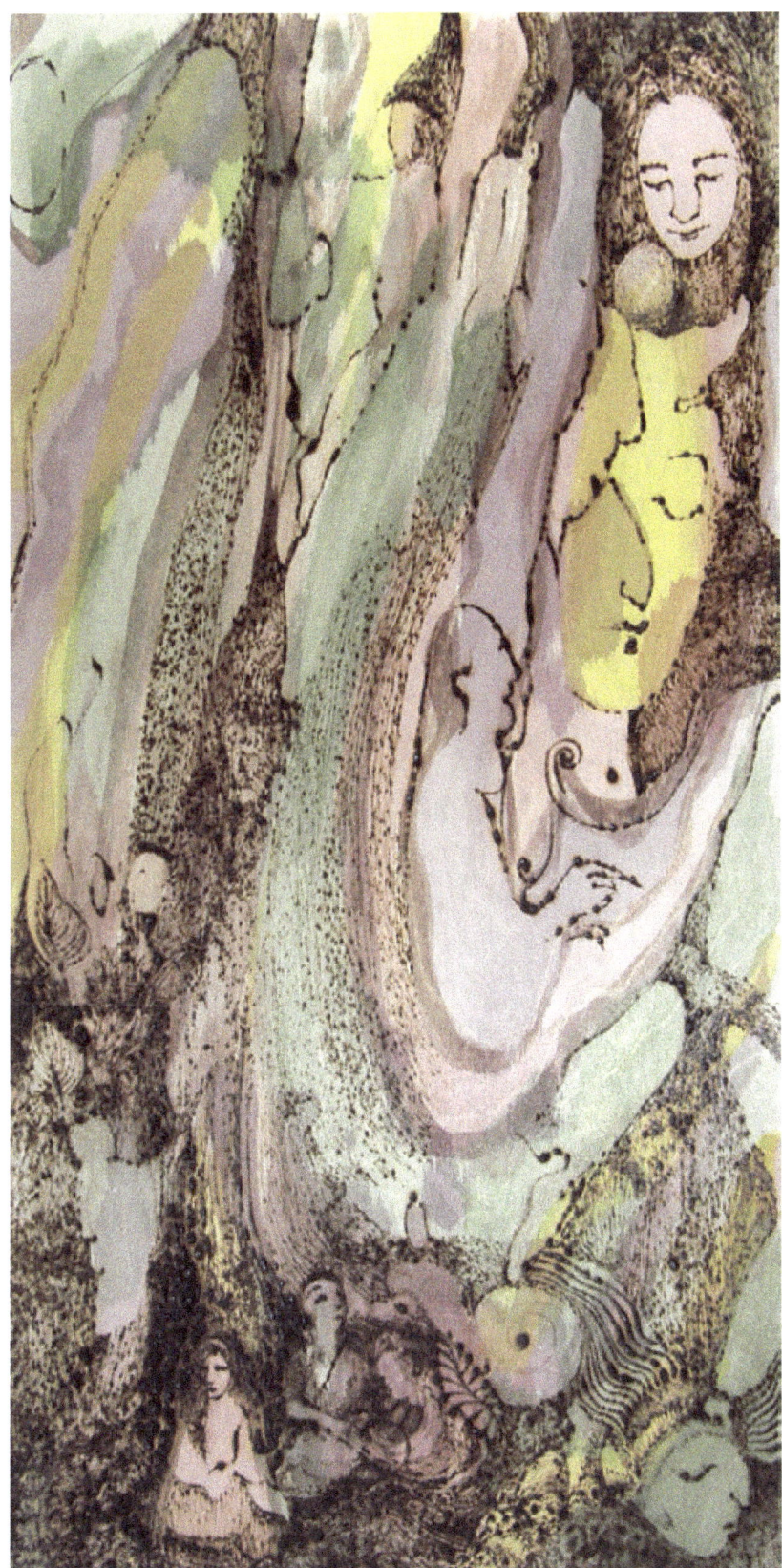

CREATING

Q: How do you cultivate you?
A: _____

Plunging deeply into blue abysmal waters,
Ebbing, flowing waves wash up a nautilus shell,
Ashore, at rest, but look within its spiral, labyrinthine walls,
Come close and hear the ceaseless call that echoes--Surrender!

Listening, listening, listening with intent,
Clinging to voices far and near
Sounds meld into a laced, song of mystery,
Soft symphonious notes, released for all to hear.

Yet few will dare to question
From where this passion rises.
What if instead, we all awoke and walked with limitless fire?
Would we fear its sprawling flames? Its full consumption? And
altering aims?

Letting go creates the space,
For expression, invention, and play for pure delight
Revealing profits beyond numbers, we humbly unite,
With a hidden astral energy that transforms dark to light.

Familiar faces, like sun and moon fill the Creating tree,
That spur community branches and spark creative endeavors.
Alone on a limb, a child takes in, the sky's changing colors,
Yellow, green, and pink, he thinks, about the true meaning of life.

Music, dance, and poetry, continue on through **dreams,**
As sun, fire, and water, cycle through their stories
We chance upon a vast, vista of beauty, and hear,
Arcadian voices living, amongst the spirited trees...

Wendy Black Nasta

It is a teeth-chattering December morning and my breath leaves a trail of cloudy puffs mid-air as I walk up the front porch. I arrive at Wendy Black Nasta's historic, Italianate villa-style home in Middletown, Connecticut, (which she believes may have been a slave safe house stop on the Underground Railroad during the 1800s). Her husband, Robert, opens the front door, leads me to the kitchen, and offers a cup of orange spice tea. I do not know Wendy well and like many of the other trailblazers featured in this book, became connected to her through a myriad of other connections. When I first explained the Spirited Trees project to her and that its purpose is to promote community and peace, Wendy immediately responded by saying, "I stand for community and peace and would love to be a part of your project."

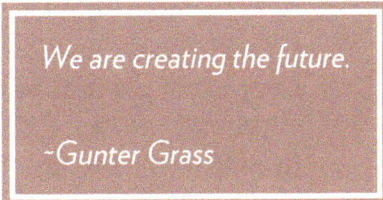

We are creating the future.

~Gunter Grass

Wendy is a successful artist, jewelry designer, peace activist, and founder of the non-profit organization, Artists for World Peace. She comes from and is part of an extensive family of artists and educators: her mother is a painter, her father a teacher, her grandfather a violinist, her uncle a pianist, her husband a world music professor and composer, her eldest son a historian, and her youngest son a drummer.

As Wendy makes her way into the kitchen, I am immediately struck once again by her multicultural features—hazel eyes, full lips, apple cheeks, and a thick mane of flowing auburn hair. She views herself as a being composed of many different religions, races, and roots, including Jewish, Native American Indian, Lithuanian, Polish, Austrian, and Mongolian. Her voice is smooth and strong as she begins to tell me about her life's journey and how she finds herself where she is today.

Wendy:
"I've traveled all over the world, but Tanzania is my favorite place; my last trip there was amazing! Tanzania, in particular, has taught me that peace work is all about giving. When we eliminate the concept of receiving, or expecting something in return for having done something, true receiving returns to us. I haven't always been this open. I used to be very judgmental. But the older I get, the more accepting I become, and am learning to embrace similarities rather than focus on differences. The more I see the world, the more I discover myself. It's like cracking open a door to see what's behind it, which reminds me of a time when I was in my late teens living in Armstrong Grove in northern California. I went there to develop my art and didn't know anyone. On weekends, I would escape to the redwood forests by myself with my guitar, sketchbook, and lantern. I was so frightened at night, but as time went on, I began to feel more comfortable. Once, I found a tree that had been so severely struck by lightning that I was able to walk inside because its trunk had been burnt out hollow. I literally was able to live in the body of that tree! That experience later inspired a line of jewelry in which I sculpted women coming out of leaves and trees. It was a popular collection that sold well at Saks Fifth Avenue. But not all of my work fared so well, like my Corrosion line from the 1970s, which was my social statement against nuclear power plants. I have always been an activist and was arrested many times at anti-war, civil rights, and environmental protests. Put it this way, I have always made my voice heard! But after having been arrested so many times and not being effective, I decided to channel my voice through my work, so the Corrosion line was born. It was beautiful: Gold and silver spheres represented the earth with acid eating away at them, which represented

the nuclear reactors. Within each sphere was a gemstone that represented hope. Everyone loved the pieces, but when I began talking about them (which to me was the absolute truth), no one bought them. I learned a valuable lesson about putting myself out there and how others will judge you. I didn't want to compromise my beliefs so that others would accept me or my work. It made me realize that people can still see your creative expression as beautiful even though they may not agree or understand you. There will always be people who support you and those that disagree with you, but we can make peace even with those that disagree with us."

> No kind action ever stops with itself. One kind action leads to another. Good example is followed. A single act of kindness throws out roots in all directions, and the roots spring up and make new trees. The greatest work that kindness does to others is that it makes them kind themselves.
>
> ~Amelia Earhart

What is valuable anyway? Our lives, our time, our health, our home, our art, our earth, our beliefs, our loved ones? How can we place a value on that which is priceless? For Wendy, it was old coins. When Europe converted its currencies to the euro in 2002, she received a phone call out of the blue from a local reporter asking how she would integrate all of the out-of-circulation European money into her artwork. The reporter had called four artists who lived and worked in Connecticut. Wendy was the only one that would make use of the coins, all the others worked with the paper currency. That phone call would end up changing not only Wendy's life, but also the many lives of people all over the world.

> No one has yet realized the wealth of sympathy, the kindness and generosity hidden in the soul of a child. The effort of every true education should be to unlock that treasure.
>
> ~Emma Goldman

She thought about the coins and envisioned a belt in which different national coins would connect to represent world peace. In addition to European currency, Wendy and her assistants began collecting coins from many other countries and in 2003, the International Peace Belt was completed. Weaving a sterling silver link chain as the base, Wendy soldered the dangling currency from the chain and added precious gemstones. Her intention was to release the belt into the world and have it travel from country to country. The belt first journeyed to India for the Golden Jubilee of World Peace and Harmony. With that event, she established her non-profit organization whose mission is to spread peace by supporting humanitarian projects in places where The International Peace Belt ventures.

Dancers, singers, musicians, poets, activists...basically all types of people from all over the world, who believe that world peace is possible have been honored to wear the belt. From Ground Zero in New York City to the Amazon Rainforest in Peru, from a Buddhist monastery in Vietnam to a Maasai tribe in Tanzania, the belt is making its way around the globe.

Listening to Wendy's story of how the peace belt was created sends chills through me. "Where is it now?" I ask. "It's here," she tells me with excitement in her eyes. She brought back the belt to solder on a coin that had fallen off. We stand up together and she leads me to another room to show me. Holding its coins and gemstones, inspecting the many faces and textures, I am in awe at the numerous places represented and how old some of the coins actually are. I finally place the peace belt against my waist.

Wendy:
"I have seen amazing things happen when people put the belt on; they feel its power and are moved to take further action for peace. When Vietnam Veterans asked to wear the belt, they brought it to a monastery where Thich Quang Duc, a Buddhist monk, had burnt himself in protest of the war. Once there, they asked the monks to bless the belt—a palpable feeling of forgiveness filled their hearts. When the belt came back to me, at least twenty-five of the gemstones had turned completely black. The stones were charred as if they had died to cleanse themselves of the war's violent energy. I've never experienced anything like that before. At another peace belt event, a group of dancers from all over the world came together and I remember a Muslim dancer saying, 'If we were home in our own countries, we could have never been able to hold hands and make peace like this.' It is ironic that these coins, which no longer have monetary value, have helped create a foundation that has given back so much from our local community to communities all over the world. We ask those who wear the peace belt to let us know if they are aware of any children who need assistance. We hold concerts, like One Concert, One Child, which is organized by my husband to raise money and awareness for our organization. Artists for World Peace sponsors eleven children—one from India, one from Haiti, and nine from Africa, who are chosen based on need. We support them financially so they have food, clothes, and an education through high school. We are now looking to see if we can sponsor them to have a college education in the United States. The youngest child we've sponsored was fourteen days old and the oldest was thirteen years old. We began sponsoring children in 2003, and I remember the first child so clearly. He was a Tibetan refugee living in India that we placed in a private academy in Moshi. My wish is to bring all of the children here to America to meet each other, to know that they are children of peace. They call me 'Mamma Wendy!'"

I love that! The program is growing with the construction of orphanages, schools, and safe houses, and with the distribution of micro-loans so that communities can buy farm animals and start small businesses. One of my favorite projects is the shoe project, where we send five hundred pairs of shoes to needy children on every continent every year. This project started because of a conversation I had with another artist friend who had worked in the Ecuadorian rainforest. She told me how the indigenous children have to walk miles and miles on dirt roads to get to school and most of them can't do it because they don't have shoes. How awful that a group of children are being denied an education because their families can't afford shoes? This was something we could help with, so got on it right away. Seeing their mouths widen into big smiles and watching them jump around after they've laced up a new pair of shoes cracks your heart open. Everyone should experience being on the other side of a child receiving his or her first pair of shoes at least once in their life. It changes your life forever. I've become great friends with a woman named Josephine who runs an orphanage in Tanzania. I've fallen in love with the people, the children, the country – they are so joyful. They have nothing, yet they have everything. They dance! They just love to dance! When I was there just a few days ago, a cancer survivor wore the peace belt. And all of a sudden everyone from the village came out and formed a circle and started singing and dancing. I have a video that you have to see!"

Wendy takes out her laptop and plays the video of this spontaneous eruption of peace. The rhythm of their voices singing and their hands clapping creates a hypnotic chorus, and even though I do not understand their words, I feel their hearts. Wendy translates their words: "Even if you have burdens that break your back, give thanks, work for peace, our prayers carry us. You work with your heart and your back..."

"I'm just scratching the surface," Wendy says. "Some days I feel frustration because there is still so much work to do..."

She may have a lot more to do, but it seems everything Wendy touches contains a living, breathing, creative spirit that ignites a cyclical chain reaction of support, a bond that is healing and helping so many all over the world grow through peace and human kindness.

CONCLUSION

CONCLUSION

"There is still so much work to do." Wendy's last comment resonates deeply with me and with others. But with our health, economic, education, and environmental systems in constant crisis, we can become paralyzed and not know where or how to begin to make even the slightest effort to illicit change.

> Walking, I am listening to a deeper way. Suddenly all my ancestors are behind me. Be still, they say. Watch and listen. You are the result of the love of thousands.
>
> -Linda Hogan

Fortunately, we can learn from example, watching those, who in their darkest hours find a way, like the elderly woman who was trapped under a pile of immovable rubble in Haiti after the devastating 2011 earthquake. For six days, not knowing how or if she would survive, she sang a song of praise and courage. She gave her life purpose even in the darkest moment and survived. It is at times like this, when we begin sifting through what is left, that we begin to see the light streaming through the cracks. That light can become a binding force that effectively makes broken people whole. That light can inspire us to keep going, even when the rubble all around us seems impenetrable.

Like trees, we grow in light. We are physical, intellectual, and spiritual beings capable of spectacular force and deeds. Feeding our spiritual component allows compassion to spring forth and nurture the ground, resulting in the most wondrous of miracles, like surviving an earthquake wreckage, or building a peaceful community amongst warring people, or giving a child living in abject poverty a pair of shoes so he may now attend school.

Thank you for walking through this forest with me, for listening to these hope-filled stories of Spirited Trees. I hope you become inspired to offer your wonderfully unique talents and gifts, to listen to the pulse of your own sweet song, and to effectively "be the change you wish to see in the world." I hope you are inspired to plant a tree, nurture it well, and watch it blossom into an extraordinary symbol of life.

Our echoes roll from soul to soul,
And grow for ever and for ever.
~Lord Alfred Tennyson

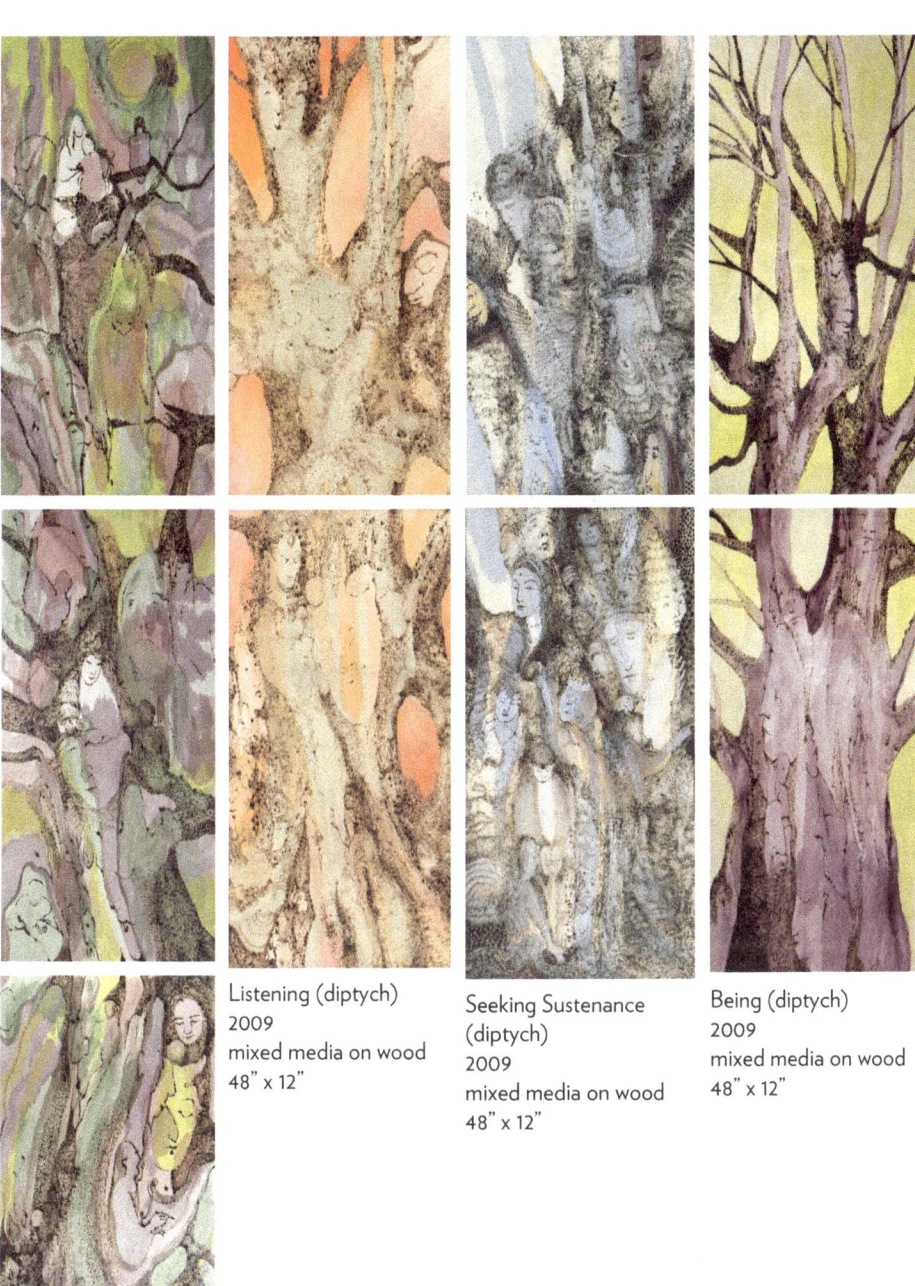

Listening (diptych)
2009
mixed media on wood
48" x 12"

Seeking Sustenance
(diptych)
2009
mixed media on wood
48" x 12"

Being (diptych)
2009
mixed media on wood
48" x 12"

Creating (triptych)
2009
mixed media on wood
72" x 12"

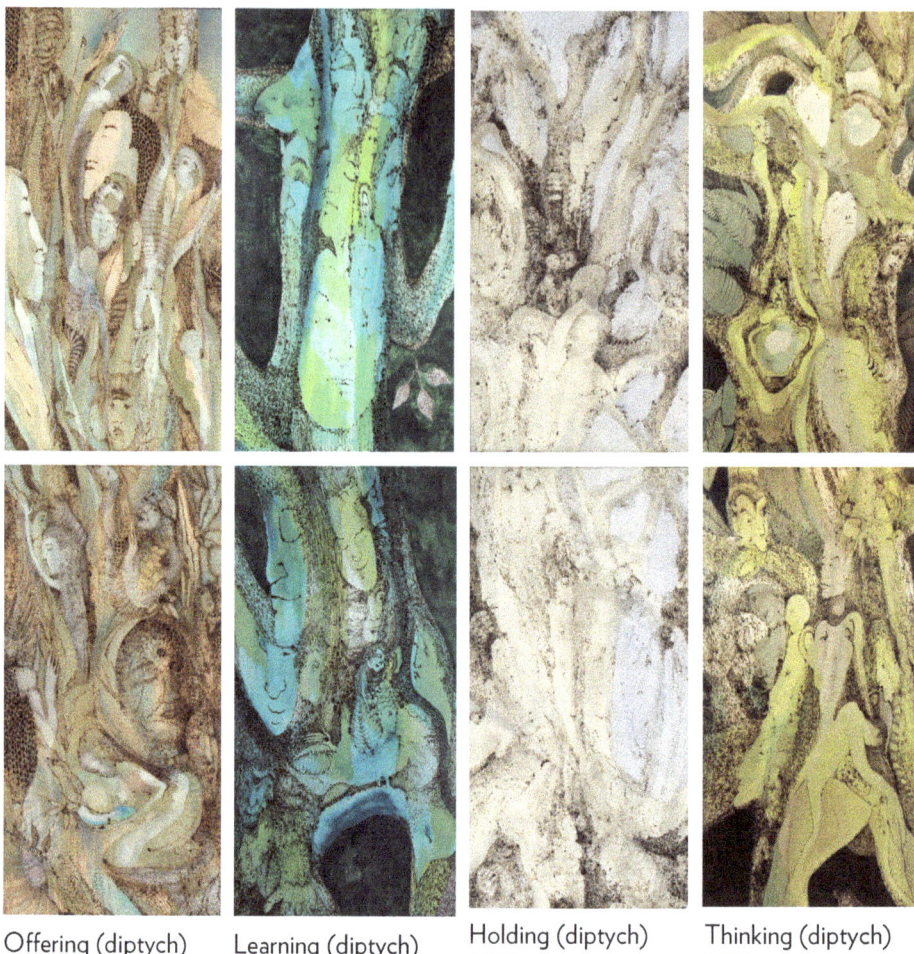

Offering (diptych)
2009
mixed media on
wood
48" x 12"

Learning (diptych)
2009
mixed media on
wood
48" x 12"

Holding (diptych)
2009
mixed media on
wood
48" x 12"

Thinking (diptych)
2009
mixed media on
wood
48" x 12"

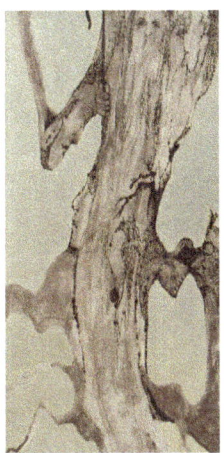 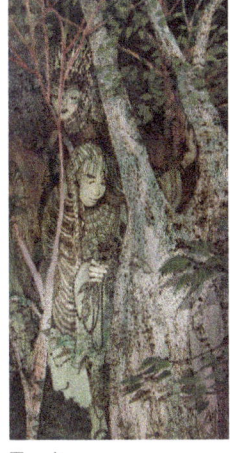 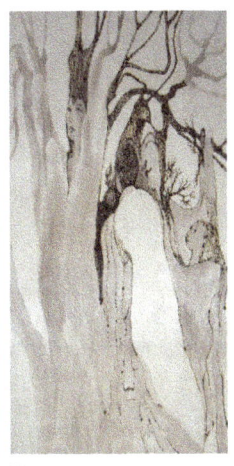

Arriving
2009
mixed media on wood
24" x 12"

Tending
2009
mixed media on wood
24" x 12"

Receiving
2009
mixed media on wood
24" x 12"